Acknowledgements

To Ashley - Who was there for me in my

This book would not have been written without the support of a range ...ations and individuals. First and foremost is DC Thomson and Mr Murray in particular who has enabled me to access the records of the Company and for the services of willing David Powell and his staff for which I am extremely grateful. To Sir Pete Downes, Principal of University of Dundee and his wonderful member of staff Peggy Hughes who have enabled me to have the Book Launch in the University. The literary talents of Eddie Small helped in taking the Book forward I will be forever grateful for his expertise. My thanks also to Mr Bruce Kelly for allowing me to tell his harrowing story which must have been extremely difficult to do. The book as I said could not have been completed without the advice of certain individuals and the determination and business acumen of Derek Shaw and Gloria was crucial in making the project a reality. My Grandsons Graham and John James supplied me with all the technical expertise and wizardry that allowed me to produce the finished article and I am grateful for their patience. Last but not least, Pauline Martin, who's artistic talents created my portrait in the City Chambers, and adorns the front cover of the book.

I am grateful to Colonel JR Hensman MBE, DL, MLITT for his extremely generous Introduction a real life hero if there ever was one, who has given the Author some credibility. I would like to thank close friend David Strachan for his expertise and knowledge for some of the interesting and authentic history of the Whitehall Theatre. My grateful thanks goes to Peter Leyland for his patience and understanding in my many changes to the book, and finally to my good friend Dr Joe Morrow for his sound and honest advice not only in the book but throughout all the years, privately and politically.

Dedication

I dedicate this book to my dear late wife Bette who steered us through our lives, the good times and the bad, She was indeed a beautiful human being who put others before herself, and although she was not with us on that eventful day at the Palace, I hope with all my heart she is aware of that, and still watching over us.

Copyright © 2016 John Letford

All rights reserved. This book or any portion thereof may not be reproduced or used in any manner whatsoever without the express written permission of the publisher except for the use of brief quotations in a book review.

Printed in Scotland by PDQ Print Services - First Printing, 2016

ISBN 978-0-9552928-3-5

Published by: PDQ Print Services, 93 Commercial Street, Dundee DD1 2AF
www.pdqprint.co.uk

Copyright © all images courtesy of DC Thomson & Co Ltd unless otherwise stated

JOHN LETFORD MBE

CITIZEN OF CREDIT AND RENOWN

In those days of blissful (for me anyway) childhood and imaginative education we learnt a poem a week. It was then, about the age of seven, I was first introduced to John Gilpin.

"John Gilpin was a citizen of credit and renown,

A trained Band Captain eke was he of famous London Town."

At that tender age I learnt about citizenship and more important, what constituted a 'good citizen', and that 'credit' and 'renown' were characteristics worthy of ambition, but that had to be earned. What 'eke' was, or what it was worth, I was not so sure! I also learned, later in life, that my own precious Royal Marines, 350 years before, were formed from those very same Trained Bands of London. So, deep in my inner conscience, a 'Citizen of Credit and Renown' was definitely bound to be 'a good egg'!

Some 50 years later, as a retired Royal Marines Officer and enjoying a second career as a crown servant supporting Reserves and Cadets in Scotland, I actually met one such Citizen! John Letford became Lord Provost of Dundee in 2001 and served his city for a record - breaking 11 years. In my book you would not qualify for this appointment unless you were an outstanding citizen in the first place. To continue in that office for more than one term would need herculean properties of honesty, integrity, not to mention energy; but to survive it for 11 years on end - that is something! I think one needs to take into account that the 90's were definitely a time of enormous change. That greatest socialist experiment of all time, the Soviet Union had just collapsed. In the UK Old Labour had become New Labour, and the stirrings of Scottish Nationalism were becoming more than just a whisper. It was a time when the reputation of politicians, both national and local, was being questioned. If ever there was a time for politicians to know what they believed I, and to stand for those beliefs - then this was it. We certainly needed citizens of credit and renown!

And it was during his time as Lord Provost that I had the honour (and the pleasure) to know him best. As one of the leading military men in the City, I had many contacts with him, both as Lord Provost and as Lord Lieutenant. The lovely thing about Scotland, and Dundee in particular, is the high regard that all Scots have for their soldiers - especially the Black Watch! Certainly John Letford is no exception. He has always loved any contact with the Armed Forces and has supported us throughout his active life. He has been a Veterans' Champion for Dundee, as Lord Lieutenant he was ex-officio President of the Soldiers, Sailors, Airmen and Families Association, and he has stayed on as our Patron well into retirement. His fantastic fund raising skills have come to the fore, and with that incredible private army of Margaret Mather, Bruce Kelly, Vic Herd and Bill Naismith, he has raised thousands of pounds for injured ex-servicemen and their families, through the annual Caird Hall Concert.

Now, I am not a politician, and it will surprise neither John himself nor any who know me, that I am not your actual Labour or SNP voter! But I did recognize the courage (and the pain) involved in his resignation from his beloved Labour Party, recounted in Chapter 11. As I said earlier, these were difficult and changing times, and this decision was not only very courageous, but wise, long sighted and served the City extremely well. We should all be very grateful to him for this selfless act. But I am a professional soldier and qualities of honour, decency, integrity and consistency are essential elements of the life itself. To be honest it is often disappointing that one does not find it more often in the political arena! More important, courage to a soldier simply defines the man, and like all those other qualities, it is especially encouraging when you find it in a career politician. John Letford is not only a remarkable politician - he is a remarkable man. As you read through his life story, you cannot help but remark on how many of these fine qualities reveal themselves; and standing clear above them all are his loyalty to his friends and family, his City, his Monarch, and his Love for Scotland and the Scottish soldier, and of course for his late wife Bette.

Jake Hensman

CONTENTS

IT'S AMAZING WHAT YOU CAN MANAGE IN A DAY

I remember that was the thought that ran through my mind as I sat in my home in Dundee after a very long, but very proud day. It was Wednesday 7th November 2012 and I had received an MBE for services to local government at Buckingham Palace earlier that day, and as I travelled down to London and back in one day you can understand that I was quite tired yet my mind was still really active.

Not that I had been alone on that journey, my three sons and my daughter had travelled with me. They had been present in the audience at the Palace, and I know it was a special day for them as it was for me. But there was a bit of sadness which tinged our day. My family was not quite complete, for Betty, their mother, and my wife of almost 54 years, had passed away in June 2009. And I knew, and I made sure they did too, that without Betty, and without her patience and understanding, her support and great common sense, this award may never have come about. Betty would have loved sharing that day with her family.

What made it even more special for me was that the Princess Royal had been the one to present my award to me. I have always been an unashamed Royalist, and have been privileged in my lifetime to have met many of the royal family, but Princess Anne was always my favourite and as this was maybe the eighth or ninth time we'd met, this helped to make me less nervous and we passed a few words of recognition as she congratulated me. That moment itself passed all too quickly; there were lots of people getting awards that day and the whole ceremony is conducted with practised military efficiency.

Speaking to some of the others before the event was enlightening because there were interesting people from all walks of life. I knew my family was seated in the main hall, witnessing the ceremony, while we, waiting in a kind of anti-room, we were called out, around five or six at a time, to await our turn. Once I had received my award I was escorted to a seat in the room to watch the presentations to all the recipients who were still to be called. I sat there, separate, but in the same room, as my sons and daughter. At this moment I began to think over the events of the day so far, and then to think of my own journey through my personal life and my civic life, and to the City and the events which led to me being in Buckingham Palace.

Those thoughts prompted and inspired the writing of this book. I felt that some of the names and the places, good and bad, deserved to be recalled because each and every one of them were influential in shaping me and in determining my pathway. The one thing I promised myself as I embarked on this book was that I would be honest and forthright in all that I wrote, and that I would take all the controversies and the victories, the happy times and the sad, and treat them with the same candour. The one common denominator which flows throughout my story is the City of Dundee-the place I served with pride has served me very well.

FAE THE BOATYAIRD TO BUCKINGHAM PALACE

I've chosen to call this book Fae the Boatyaird to Buckingham Palace, because I think that sums up the remarkable journey my life has taken. Not that it was all a planned and trouble-free jaunt through the years; it was anything but. Like almost all people I've had to cope with life's trials and tribulations, and whilst I've made my own decisions throughout my life, some things do come about by happenstance and sometimes I've simply had to ride out the waves. The story that follows will describe that journey, and along the way I'll tell you things that I've never mentioned to a soul before, and I will also open up details on some of the unpublicised episodes in my political and private lives. The distance between Dundee's Boatyaird and London's Buckingham Palace is a long one in miles, and even further in social terms, but, of course, I had a life before I arrived at 'The Boatyaird' and this first chapter will take me through my childhood.

The city of Dundee is a special place for me and my feelings about the town are as warm and strong now as they have ever been. Even today I still feel a thrill when I enter Dundee after being away somewhere. But it's not only Dundee that holds special memories for me – the thrill I get when I go to Glasgow is in many ways the same, if not maybe quite as strong. Both these Scottish cities have similarities which appeal to me, and each, in its own way, and at different times, played a big part in my life and my upbringing. I suppose you could say I get a warm feeling of belonging in each of these great Scottish cities.

But I must tell you that Aberdeen, too, has an effect on me - not as much as Dundee, but strong nevertheless, and this is because Aberdeen is the place where I was born.

On 5th March, 1935, I became my parents' third child. My older brother, David, was nearly 7 years old, and my sister, Irene, was 5 at the time. We lived in Holburn Street, although I obviously can't remember it. It was in a really nice and desirable area of Aberdeen, but our housing arrangements would change for the worse shortly after. My earliest memories of Aberdeen revolve around the Second World War black-outs. I can vividly remember the exodus of people fleeing from our tenement building heading for the warrens of air-raid shelters in the 'backies' behind Castle Street just off Union Street. The wailing of the air-raid sirens brought a sense of fear and nervous excitement to me, and to just about everyone, and of all the memories that wartime evokes, this is one of the strongest. The area today houses a large retail clothing store, but at that time it was just a stone's throw from the fish docks that were so important to the city's economy. I remember, too, that my father chose to stay in his bed during one particular bombing raid.

I especially recall that night in 1942 when a German Bomber unloaded a bomb in Aberdeen Harbour. I was seven at the time, and we believed that he dropped his bomb on the way home from attacks on shipping. Apparently Aberdeen was the most frequently attacked of Scottish cities and suffered around twenty-eight separate bombing raids, but Fraserburgh too had to put up with a lot. The proximity of North-East Scotland to the Norwegian airbases used by the Germans was part of the reason. Why I remember the raid of 1942, and not the more deadly one in 1943 that claimed 125 lives, is probably because it was so close to our home. And that memory of my father staying in his bed was possibly the last memory I have of him because he left our family home later that same year.

When I was born we were, it seems, a happy family. My father was also called John. He'd been born in Glasgow in 1908 and by the time he was twenty he had met and married my mother. Records show they married in Whale Place in Aberdeen on the 25th August, 1928. At the time of their marriage, my father worked on the farms, but by 1935, when I came along, he was a Fish Carter, a job that many men in Aberdeen did at the time. My mother's name was Catherine and she'd been born in Banchory in Aberdeenshire in 1900, so she was a good bit older than my father. I don't know what took my father up to Aberdeen from his family in Glasgow. Whether he was looking for work there during the depression which so crippled Glasgow, or whether he'd met my mother somewhere and moved to be with her, is something we'll never know, but things seem to have been going along well. However, everything was to change radically for us soon after I came along.

My brother tells me that our mother got into an argument one day with a man who was one of our neighbours. This was apparently about nothing more serious than whose turn it was to use the communal drying area in the back green, but the man was quite verbally abusive. When my father came home, and was told of this fracas, he was livid, and he proceeded to go and speak to this neighbour. Apparently my father knocked the neighbour about, and as a result he was charged by the police and we were evicted from our home in a well-respected area and ended up living in the most deplorable conditions imaginable. At that time, in most cities and towns, there were areas of old and ill-equipped housing, but in reality the 'new' house was barely inhabitable. Sanitation was primitive and dreadful, and the tenement building, and indeed the whole area, was populated by all kinds of 'low life'. This fact would impact directly on me in ways that I've kept to myself until now.

The first impact was the fact that my mother and father split up. This was in 1942, and I have no memory of it, but my brother David thinks it was triggered by my father's repugnance at the disgusting conditions we were now living in. The irony of this is that we were forced to move there because of his violent attack on that neighbour. My mother and father never did get together again, but, for whatever reason, they never did divorce each other either. Their separation had repercussions for us all, and we would be split up as a family for a while, but the second impact of the move to the tenement from Hell was something that involved only me.

I remember the incident very clearly, as though it was only yesterday. I was seven years old at the time when I was sexually and physically abused by one of our neighbours. My sister, Irene, told me the man's name a long time after it happened. He was called Stevie Stopper, and he was a disabled man. Apparently he suffered deserved retribution at the hands of neighbours before being carted off by the police, and he was never seen in our neighbourhood again. I suppose it might have been even worse than it was, but this left an indelible mark on me to the extent that I've never told my own family about it to this day. I found this episode in my life was too embarrassing to share with them, and I can only surmise that many others who have been in the same situation have felt exactly the same. When they read this my children will be shocked, but when you've bottled something like that up for over seventy years it's not easy to let it go.

After the separation of my parents, my mother was forced to put her children into the homes of relatives. This was wartime, and many families had their children evacuated, so there was no apparent stigma in splitting up, and, as a result, I was parcelled off to be looked after by my father's sister, my Aunt Mary, in Glasgow, whilst David and Irene were less lucky and were sent together to a home in Aberdeenshire which they managed to 'escape from' on a couple of occasions. I obviously fared better than my siblings because I was seemingly 'spoilt rotten' in Aunt Mary's house in Gayfield Street in Glasgow. This street was demolished in the building of the M8 motorway, but although I was only a nipper I can remember the building was a lovely tenement, although after our hovel in Aberdeen I suppose most places would seem wonderful.

Destined for the RAF - aged 5?

Aunt Mary was the third child of eleven to my grandfather, Robert Letford from Kirkintilloch. His first seven children, including my father who was the sixth, had Mary Ann Queen Letford for their mother, but she sadly died in January 1911 of consumption (Phthisis Pulmonalis is the fancy name on the Death Certificate). Robert was married again in Glasgow by June of the same year to Mary Quigley. My grandfather's second wife gave birth to Hugh, their first child together, in March 1912, and she gave birth in the same bed in Westerhill Street, Glasgow, in which my grandmother, Mary Ann, had died two years earlier.

I can conjure up one specific memory of meeting my grandfather, but I remember it very well. He owned a coal delivery business at the time, and he had a yard with coal-carts, and stables for his horses, but my clearest recollection is of the two massive Alsatian dogs that were constantly at his side. A dear late friend of mine called Margaret Thomson, who had once walked all the way from Glasgow to Dundee to marry her beloved Hugh, knew my grandfather much better, and she told me of his 'terrible' reputation for being a man who liked the ladies. Money was in short supply for many people in those days, and a bag of coal was essential but not cheap, so it was well known that Robert Letford (Rab) would sometimes accept 'payment in kind'. I mentioned this in the Evening Telegraph column that I regularly wrote, and even today my thoughts of Margaret, and of her tales about my grandfather, make me smile warmly. Whatever his faults though, my grandfather was clearly a hard-working man who provided for his eleven children and two wives, and he reached the grand age of 86 before he died of cancer of the liver and prostate in 1964 at his then home in Edgefauld Road in his beloved hometown. A 'Glasgow' man through all his days, he served his country during the First World War as a soldier in the 9th Battalion of the Cameron Highlanders, and I like to think that part of my own work ethic and regard for the military has seeped down to me from his genes.

My time in Glasgow with Aunt Mary was reasonably short-lived, amounting to around a year or so, but I well-remember her kindness. Her house had a niche in the wall where I slept, and Mary's sister, my Aunt Becky, used to give me a toffee apple from time to time from the batches she made and sold round the neighbours. I remember, still, the smell and the taste of those apples, but strangely I have no recollection at all of going to school in Glasgow. I suppose I did, but it's a true saying that we always remember the good things best on looking back. And now I think of it, I can also remember Mary had hair that could almost reach the floor. She had a daughter, Catherine, who must have been about school leaving age when I stayed there, and Cathie seemed to be about six foot tall. Seeing mother and daughter together must have been amusing for I can remember it still. All too soon it was time for me to go back to Aberdeen.

My memories of my return to Aberdeen are sketchy, but this reunion was to be quite short lived. One day I was helping my sister with her milk delivery job when I fell off the horse-drawn float. I landed under the float, and the uncaring horse proceeded to pull the float over my legs resulting in me being hospitalised. I had a broken right leg and a crushed left hand, and my recuperation culminated in me being 'transferred' to Coultra Farm, near Gauldry in Fife, where I was to stay with my Aunt Annie and Uncle Duncan. Annie was my mother's half-sister, and I remember with great fondness my time with her and her husband Duncan, and their large family of Willie, Donald, Duncan, Robert, Stan, Jean, Gladys, Barbara, Peggy and Lily. I found life on the farm to be absolutely brilliant, and I've no doubt it helped my recuperation enormously, but whether it helped my education is less certain. I was enrolled in Gauldry Primary School, which was around three miles from the farm, and I walked daily, along with Stan and Lily, there and back. There was a school-bus which passed the farm, but the operators, Williamsons of Gauldry, maintained that we did not qualify for free travel, and so the bus would pass us twice daily as we trudged along in all kinds of weather. Uncle Duncan decided to test the waters legally about this, and I can well remember him telling us that if the bus passed us on this particular morning we should turn around and proceed back to the farm in which case he would instigate court proceedings. I can still picture the 'Three Musketeers' walking to school that day, hoping and praying that the bus wouldn't stop, and lo and behold our prayers were answered when the bus sallied on by as usual. We were happy in the extreme, and we remained happy for the next twelve months until Uncle Duncan won his court case and we lost our freedom and resumed our education.

My days at Coultra Farm provided an important and thoroughly enjoyable time in my life. I became aware of tractors – not something that many 'townies' would know about - and I came to recognise the places that Shire horses could get to places where a tractor couldn't. I remember the German prisoners-of-war, a regular site around farms, who each wore a big red spot on the back of their jackets. I recall hunting for rabbits with Duncan's two dogs, Jackie and Poopa, and the rabbit stew we ate most days which attested to the dogs' ability. Aunt Annie never ceased to amaze me in her ability to skin a rabbit, which she would have hanging on the kitchen door beforehand. All these sights and sounds come back to me clearly when I think back to those days, but there was one occasion, when I remembered them especially.

In my capacity of Lord Provost of Dundee I was attending a dinner in the City Chambers that we were hosting for Friends of Camperdown. I had the good fortune to be sitting next to Janet Fox-Pitt, who was the sculptor of the statue to Admiral Duncan which sits grandly outside St Pauls Cathedral in Dundee. We exchanged family stories, and I mentioned my time at Coultra Farm. The astonishing thing was that Janet's mother, Lady Patricia of Dundee, was now the present occupant. Janet assured me her mother would be pleased to meet me, and, sure enough, a short time later I received a formal invitation to visit the place which meant so much in my childhood. I was graciously received, and my wonderment at the changes filled me with delight. It was indeed a far cry from the days of no electricity, of no running water, and of having to chop down trees by hand to supply logs for the fire. Yet despite the stark contrast between now and then I still consider this to have been a great place for a youngster to be brought up in.

For some reason that I can't recall, my aunt and uncle decided to leave Coultra, and cross to the north side of the Tay where they took on Whitewalls Farm, Emmock Road, Tealing. My most vivid memory of Whitewalls was the severe winter of 1947. The snow lay higher than the farm fence-posts, exciting for a twelve-year-old, and we all mucked in to dig out snow blocks on the dirt track that ran between the farm and the main road. This was essential because the grocery van was there to deliver the food supplies that kept us all alive. My second most abiding memory of the stay at Whitewalls concerns a monkey. Incredible as it sounds, my Aunt Annie owned a Blue Monkey, and you don't get many of them in Tealing. It used to hold the farm cats between its legs and debug their fur of all the creepie-crawlies that sometimes inhabit farm animals. But the monkey had a malicious side too, and I remember an occasion when my brother David left his violin in the custody of Annie for safe-keeping. The Blue Monkey got a hold of the instrument and smashed it to pieces, and we didn't have the heart to tell David so he was told that the violin had 'disappeared'. It took me 66 years, when David came for a visit to Dundee from his home in his adopted country of Australia, to pluck up the courage and tell him the real truth about his blessed violin.

My schooling at Tealing was at Den of Mains School just on the edge of Dundee. The school had a tin roof and it was cold in wintertime. It was the smallest school in Dundee, according to Dundee Corporation who owned it at the time, and my one memorable achievement when

I was there was lifting the Burns Federation prize. Apparently the Burns Federation supplied a prize, usually a book of poetry, to many schools for this poetry-reading and singing competition, and I was fair chuffed to win it given my patchy education and nomad existence. The end of my Primary School days brought with it an end to my days of living in the countryside. I had to move to Logie Secondary in Dundee's Blackness Road. This school and the area it was in, was about as different from my past schools as you could imagine.

If I try hard enough I can recall some of the names from my Logie days; the Headmaster was Mr Fraser, the Maths teacher was nicknamed "Smykes" for some reason, and the Science teacher was Mr Hyslop. I remembered him best, because he ran the school football team, I played in goal for the school team, something that made me proud, but I was not the first choice "keeper", that was a lad called Stark (I think his first name was Ron or Roy) who was good enough to play for the Dundee Schoolboys- quite an accolade in days when all schools had good sides. I have a picture of our class taken in 1950 and some names threaten to come back to me when I look at it, happy days-well, some of the time!

Where Whitewalls Farm sat in the relatively remote farmlands to the north of Dundee, Logie School was located in a very densely populated area. Tenement buildings abounded in this part of Dundee, and there had always been a sense of community brought about by the close proximity between neighbours and buildings. These houses were thrown up in the late nineteenth century to accommodate people working in Dundee jute mills and other industries, and having a sense of privacy, and a feeling of space, was almost impossible after the open emptiness of Whitewalls. My new landlady was Gert McKenzie, and her home was in a tenement block at 105 Hawkhill. I presume my mother was instrumental in finding Gert, a lady who was disabled – a great drawback when you don't live on the ground floor. I have to think hard to remember very much of my stay with Gert and I suppose the local shops and the fact that ration books from the War years were still being used are the clearest things that come to mind. I must have gone for most of the messages to the local shops, and I can remember Pacione's ice cream shop, because Emilio Pacione played for Dundee United. They were a great football family and his brother, Sid, played for Aberdeen and Hibernian.

Another footballing shopkeeper, and also of Italian extract, was Peter Cabrelli. He had a chip shop at 89 Hawkhill- I can still smell the chips now- and he was a man of many football clubs. Amongst them were Falkirk, Dundee United, Dundee, Halifax Town, Millwall and Arsenal, as well as the Italian teams of Borgatoro and Ambrosiano Milan (later to become Inter Milan). But the team that probably gave him the most fun was Dundee Juventus in Dundee's esteemed Half-Holiday League. Many an excellent player came through this league which included teams of policeman, fireman, posties, and shop workers who all turned out on a Wednesday afternoon to some amazingly good crowds.

I can still picture the pubs, which always seemed busy, and all the grocer shops and the butchers, bakers and the dentist too. Hawkhill was a place full of life, and colour and hub-bub, by day and by night. There was a Bed & Breakfast place near Balfour Street Tech. that was used by many of the great Scottish Artists who were appearing in Dundee, often at the Palace Theatre behind the Queens Hotel, Jimmy Logan, Will Starr and Johnny Victory were regulars, and I can clearly remember Johnny Victory's Rolls Royce turning up at the B & B

Gert's house was always quite quiet, other than visits from her daughter and granddaughter, so while it was a world away from Whitewalls and Coutra, there was enough happening inside and outside that house to keep me from wearying. I stayed in the Hawkhill right through my Secondary School days and was still there when the time came for me to start a Pre-apprenticeship in Engineering at the Trades School in Ann Street. I think the Tech. was part of Ann Street school and the only lad I can remember from those days was called Fitchett whose family owned the milk business in Dundee (Ithink)

I still have my Trades School Report Card for 1950/51. It lists my Junior Secondary Certificate amongst my achievements, and the Head Teacher, Alex M Black, has signed the card which proclaims to anyone interested that my attendance and conduct records were excellent. My trade preference, even at that time, was in sheet metal work, and I put my good marks in the Trades School down to the love I had for this type of work.

On the death of Gert McKenzie, my mother, who was the Housekeeper at Harrison's Hotel in Dundee's Roseangle, found me an excellent new landlady by the name of Mrs Gordon. Her house was in Annfield Street, just off the 'Blackie', and not that far from Hawkhill. Nearby was the famous "Blackie" foundry and you could feel the heat of the place when you gazed in at the busy men working at their trade. Our family connection was that Mrs Gordon's son had married my cousin Gladys, Aunt Annie's daughter. My mother's hand had been there in all my moves up to this point, and though she obviously wasn't in a position to keep me herself, she did well in making sure I was cared for. I had a wonderful stay with Mrs Gordon during the years while I served my apprenticeship in the Caledon Shipyard as a Marine Coppersmith.

Looking back, I realise that many children were evacuated to other homes during the war period, and so my nomadic existence was not as extraordinary to others as it would be today. We learn from every experience, and I think my different homes with different sorts of people gave me a real grounding in life and an appreciation of all sorts of things. I never really got to know Aberdeen as a home because I was too young to appreciate things, and my stay in Glasgow, in that smashing tenement, was too short-lived to leave very many memories. My times in the farms, both South and North of Dundee, were at a time when my mind was old enough to appreciate things, and the differences between town and country life taught me so much. Both of these places were sited tantalisingly close to Dundee, and so my move there, to that long-demolished tenement flat at 105 Hawkhill, would still have been a culture shock, but at least I was old enough to make the most of things. And, of course, I was a young man when I moved in to Mrs Gordon's in Annfield Street, moving into industry with a clear eye to the future and to working with my hands in Dundee ship-building industry. During my stay there, I got word my father had died. According to the death certificate he died 'in a field' on the farm at Kincluny, Durris, Aberdeenshire. The cause of death was said to be 'natural causes - probably Coronary Thrombosis'. Later my brother told me about the funeral at Allanvale Cemetary chapel. He was there along with my sister Irene, and my mother. Apparently Uncle Dick (my father's older brother) was there, and saw to all the formalities, and David sort of remembers that one of my father's sisters, it might have been Mary or Becky, was also at the funeral. David said that they didn't go to the graveside after the service at the chapel, but went straight for a 'cup of tea' at a pub in Brig o' Dee.

I can't remember just what I thought at the time, but circumstances were what they were – if things had turned out differently with him and my mother I'm sure my feelings towards him would have been very different. I did see my brother and sister occasionally at that time, and I reckon I saw my mother most weeks during my school holidays when I was living on the Hawkhill. Whilst my time with Mrs Gordon was really good, my mind was on work, and wage-earning, and before long it would be on something else too. It would not be long until I would meet the young woman who would share my life.

"BETTE"

It all started in a snooker hall

I have to confess as to having a "misspent youth" as they say with regard to the game of snooker which I was obsessed with from about 14 years of age until I left the Royal Air Force in National Service 1958. That period of time playing snooker was very important to me, not for the snooker itself but because of it, and the reason I met my Wife to be Bette.

Bette's brother Billy was a fellow snooker player in Terry's snooker establishment in Larch St at the bottom of Danialls Brae between Blackness Rd and Brook St with Bette's house nearby in Urquhart Street and Bette started making a habit of coming to the door of the snooker hall and shouting "Billy your tea is ready" and although she denied it, I said for all the years to follow that she only came in to see me!

anyone for tea?

These meetings progressed to meeting each morning in Blackness Road, her going for the morning rolls and me walking down to town, and along Dock St to the Caledon where I served my time as a Marine Coppersmith. Two years later when 20 years of age and Bette 18 we were married in St Joseph's Church by Cannon Malloy on the 18th June 1955 with our oldest Son John born on the 29th March 1956

Our first house was 2 rooms in Temple Lane in the West Port above the Pawnshop and leaning out the window to see to see familiar faces putting their wares in on a Monday and getting them back on Friday. It was a tough life in those days. On finishing my apprenticeship in the Boatyaird and one weeks wage of £5 I was whisked off to National Service in 1956 to serve 2 years in Her Majesty's Royal Air Force at RAF Hemswell in Lincolnshire when Bette made the journey down with Son John to living out quarters in Gainsbourgh where we could all be together and I still remember the address Rectory Ave. but not the number, RAF Hemswell apparently, although I can't remember knowing about it at the time, was where they filmed the Dambusters in 1954

Prior to my "demob" Bette returned to Dundee and set up house in the high tenement in West Henderson's Wynd but it was not long before we moved on to Urquhart St. to live beside her Mum and Dad Agnes and Willie Grant where we were to stay until we got a Semi Detached in Invercraig Place Charleston now with a complete Family of John, Graham, Billy and Elizabeth who would all grow up at this address until they "flew the coop" to pursue their own lives.

When we married, Bette's Mum insisted that we get married in the Catholic Church which meant I had to have "Instruction" in the Catholic faith which in the Church's eyes made me a Convert. There were little or no problems with Bette and me religion wise and the Kids were educated in Catholic Schools except for Elizabeth who wished to attend a Secondary non- denomination School at Menziehill High which she did until leaving age. The ironic thing regarding all of this was that the boys married Protestants, brought them up in that faith and their kids obviously went to non-denomination Schools whereby Elizabeth married a Catholic and their Son John James attends St John's! It's a funny old world is it not.

Bette's was a Weaver, a noble profession and crucial to this City for over 200 years. Early pictures of Weavers regularly shows them wearing hats, and often gloves too to their work and they really were at the top of the hierarchy in the textile trade. Woe betide anyone who says or thinks a Weaver works in the Mill. The Mill was for the heavy often unskilled, aspects of jute and linen preparation, but the skilled worker, that is those involved in the finishing of the product, worked in the "factory" Bette instilled this fact in to me, and I have never forgotten it, so neither should you! There were little or no nurseries in those days, so it's off to work I go during the day and Bette

Today is God's gift to me: What I do with it is my gift to God!

found in the Keepsakes of Edith Coupar © Alex Coupar 1997

did the 5pm to 10pm shift in the evenings which saw us through the early lives of our children. I had left the snooker days behind me of course and my life revolved around football, firstly as a player, a qualified Referee, and Administrator in local football Associations before I started the Sunday Boys League which entailed Charleston Celtic later to become Dundee Celtic Boys and finally St Columba Boys Club. Bette was almost a football widow, but not quite because she supported every one of these activities that I had, washing and ironing shirts, half time hospitality for the kids, cooking meals at football dinners, fund raising and so on and then came another challenge for her the Civic Head of the City, and the Lady Provost.

Bette supported me on all these activities I have mentioned and I honestly could not have done it without her and here she was again having to make sacrifices, but this time she was being thrust into the limelight and all the responsibilities that went with it and when she said to me "John, what will I have to do and do you think I can manage? My reply was short and sweet "Bette just be yourself, that's good enough for me and will be for everyone else.

Well she did and it was, Bette worked hard in a role she was not always comfortable with and in doing what she did she was doing more than helping me carry out my duties. Her charity work and fund raising was immense particularly with the Orphans of Budimex Hospital in Romania and her thousands of pounds raised and support for Sister Aluyisis was gratefully received by the Hospital and the Catholic Church. Her help for community events was continuous and her sole efforts in the annual Best Baby Judging Events stopped me from being a hated figure in the Ferry.

Bette & I at the christening of Great-Granddaughter Kaitlyn

I cannot write my story without telling you what the real Bette was like, we had 54 years of the love and friendship she had for her family and friends her constant giving to others asking for nothing in return making sure her family had everything and leaving herself to last, she will obviously be remembered for that, but the other side that myself and the family experienced will be a joy forever and a source of fun, laughter and yes at times frustration and a sense of disbelief of what she said and did.

Let's start at her nickname of Jaws and the Godmother

Bette was a typical Dundee Wifie and I say that in the nicest possible way. She was strong, vocal, did not suffer fools gladly and no one and I mean no one was ever going to take advantage of her, particularly shop assistants who at many times will ignore you and have a blether with their mates, well, Bette had an answer for that one and her voice could be heard booming across whichever store she happened to be in "Is there nobody serving in this shop"

Her other pet hate was the traffic wardens who she affectionately nicknamed the Weasels and one day in Castle Street when a poor Warden was booking someone, not me I hasten to add, she shouted "awa an get yersel a proper job", frightened the poor man to death I can tell you.

But if the traffic wardens feared her the Civic Council Officers loved her because more than once, if we were at a function and getting dinner, she would say to me "are they not getting anything to eat?" and rather sheepishly I would say "I don't think so" she would then proceed to ask whoever was in charge if they could get a meal! Didn't always work mind you but the Council Officers appreciated her concern, other than Davy Barr of course who always preferred to go and get a fish supper

There were numerous occasions when she put her foot in it bless her and once she nearly killed a Duck down in Lancaster when her arrow at a shooting range went way off course and in to a Duck Pond, the Ducks and the Farmer were very unhappy of course

She was, of course, accident prone and one summer day down at Monifieth she set the heather on fire with a thrown away cigarette and it took myself and three others ages to carry sand back and forth to put it out

My favourite of all the mishaps that gave me and the family endless joy was on an excursion to the ruins of Pompeii on a cruise and for anyone who has been there will know what I am talking about. Bette was in a wheel chair on this particular trip but we had to alight to walk up the small road that took you up to the famous ruins. The path was as it was over 2000 years ago "cassies" and small boulders of course and was difficult to negotiate in getting to the top especially for Bette.

We got to the top eventually and she was knackered as the saying goes and on finding a seat she uttered her immortal words (now they are) "They will have to do something about that road"

You could not make that up, nor the countless other similar incidents, and I never think back without thanking Bette for these wonderful memories.

Speaking about wheel chairs, on that same trip, and to the Vatican in Rome there was no way she could walk up that steep hill so I had to do the needful and that was after we were nearly run down by a taxi in the street, we laughed about that one would you believe. It was no laughing matter in the Vatican though we found to our cost as most of the people were so rude because of the wheelchair and I learned a lesson that day about what disabled people have to endure.

The wheel chair and her sore backs was another indication that her health was getting worse but no sign that anything was wrong but the pain continued and a visit to the GP and a blood test sent her to Ninewells Hospital where she received a scan and the Doctor who shall remain nameless said there wasn't anything that gave him concern but they would do another scan to confirm this.

On our return for the results and as I entered his office he had two chairs side by side and I feared the worst, I understand the difficulty for him when he had to tell us that the scan was negative and cancer of the liver was evident and incurable, but he had only a week prior said everything was ok.

Bette took the news and her composure was unbelievable and asked the Doctor very calmly, how long she had left. By that time I had lost control completely and was of no use to her what so ever, and that was something I regretted and still regret to this very day. I started to make arrangements to resign but she was not having any of that and as she said on many occasions "you will just have to get on with it John" easier said than done.

The Doctor at Ninewells Hospital told us then that a year was about all that Bette had left, the Macmillan Nurses started to visit, and that estimate changed to months, but our GP Dr Flavahan who visited regularly warned us that days was more likely.

We sat together constantly sometimes talking, other times silent, her biggest regret she said was that she would not see her Grandchildren and Great-Grandchildren growing up and the last thing she wanted to be was an invalid.

Bette slept peacefully for some few days and passed away on the 14th June 2009 at 6.30pm in the evening, within 3 weeks after her diagnosis, with myself, our Daughter Elizabeth and our first Grandchild Leanne by her side.

BLACK WATCH

I have shared many wonderful events with the illustrious Black Watch and I remember with pride my invitation to travel down to Warminster England, the destination and holding Camp for the returning soldiers from Iraq and I was deeply honoured when asked by the Mayor of Westminster to share the Podium with him at the march past. I have welcomed the Black Watch here in Dundee on many occasions both on Parade and in the City Chambers, and have reaffirmed their Freedom of The City, but Warminster was something special. There were literally thousands in the streets to welcome our heroes return and this little English town was awash with everybody's Saltire flags and I honestly only saw a couple of Union ones, very moving indeed and following the Parade we attended a memorial service for those Black Watch who had lost their lives. I was asked by Lieutenant General Sir Alistair Irwin KCB, CBE the "High Heid Yin" if I would like to speak to the "Jocks" from Dundee who were assembled for me and it was one of the proudest moments of my life.

Balhousie Castle Perth the ancestral home of the Black Watch, was a favourite "haunt" of mine and I attended, and still do, as often as I can and my last visit was for the opening of the spectacular new Museum when I met many good friends including the Chairman of the Black Watch Heritage Trust Lieutenant General Sir Alastair Irwin who I mentioned earlier and the Black Watch Association Secretary, my Mentor Major Ronnie Proctor MBE.

I suppose the highest accolade that was bestowed on me, was to be appointed the President of the Black Watch Association when Lord Provost and I remember asking Major Proctor how big an area did that Presidency cover, and he said to me "Lord Provost, there is only one Black Watch Association so it's worldwide"

There were other great Black Watch moments during my tenure of Office and the Beret with the Red Hackle comes to mind as one I will never forget.

This particular occasion is one that will remain in my memory forever when I was invited to speak at the Annual Black Watch Association Dinner in Arthurstone Terrace Dundee on a subject of my choice, and I thought the history of the origin of the Red Hackle would be very appropriate but I will forever remember the words of Council Officer Frank Traynor, "make sure you get your facts right Lord Provost" so with Frank's advice ringing in my ears I contacted the War Museum in Edinburgh and duly received the appropriate documents. When I arrived at the Club speech in hand I spoke to the Gaffer Willie Barr telling him my speech was 10 minutes long, far too long he said "cut it" how about 8 minutes Willie I asked him "Lord Provost you are using good drinking time, 3 minutes last offer"

I ignored Willie of course and forged ahead until near the end when a drunken irate member staggered on to the floor and gave me foul and abusive language until Willie took him by the scruff of the neck and dragged him back to his seat. When I sat down to a thunderous round of applause I have to tell you, I asked my good friend Colonel Alex Murdoch what was that all about, to be told " Lord Provost, there are about five different versions of the origin of the Red Hackle and you picked the wrong one" so much for the War Museum then! I returned to the Chambers to a jubilant Council Officer and "I told you to make sure your facts were right Lord Provost"

The rich history of the Black Watch is well documented and over the years I have attended many lectures from historians and soldiers who themselves have served in this illustrious Regiment and speak with passion of their personal experiences, and such a man is my mentor and good friend Major Ronnie Proctor MBE who has guided me in my role as Lord Provost and Lord Lieutenant working together not only for the Black Watch but for the Armed Forces in general. Ronnie continues to serve the Regiment in his present and major role as Secretary of Balhousie Castle Perth and is a bit of legend throughout Scotland and beyond, Ronnie is now a conservative Councillor for the Kirriemuir area but this does not make him a bad person!

On one wonderful occasion I visited Perth to attend the launch of the Regimental history book "The Highland Furies The Black Watch 1739-1899 and there were three books presented that day signed by the Author Victoria Schofield and the third book to my astonishment and great delight was presented to me and became my prized possession.

The Highland Furies is as of course the official history of the Black Watch 1739-1899 with the follow up and final chapter to come some in the future, and the book echoes the ethos of our great Regiment and also echoes the words and deeds of Ronnie Proctor and others, who tell us of a Regiment formed in 1739 originally to 'watch' over any misdemeanours committed in our beautiful but sometimes volatile Highlands, and sanctioned by , I have to say, by the then King George 2nd, the same man who got me into trouble with my speech about the Red Hackle in the Black Watch Association Cub. The various "engagements" carried out by the Regiment across the world over the years since their formation in 1739 trips off the tongue with great ease by Veterans past and present, not only remembered for their glorious successes, but also for their many tragic losses of life in battle and they are of course feared and respected across the world no more so than in our Twinning City of Alexandria Virginia which is proud of its Scottish history, I have never plucked up the courage to tell them that the Black Watch burned down their White House in the War of Independence.

The 'Forty Second' never dies

It hath a regimental soul;

Fond Scotia, weeping, filled with blanks

Which Quatre Bras left in its roll.

At Alma, at Sevastopol,

At Lucknow, waved its bonnet blue!

Its dark green tartan, who but knows?

What heart but warms to "Forty Two!

So nearly sixty years on from my first attempt and my dream to join my beloved Black Watch, my patience has been rewarded and I have experienced untold joy that will stay with me forever.

The Black Watch did not stand alone however in my passion for the Military Services, their sacrifices, and their challenges were shared by others who fell and those who survived not only in both world wars, but in the continuing conflicts throughout the world and still claim the lives of our young people and that is why, we as a city, will always remember our hero's sacrifices and commemorate all our Remembrance Services.

Here in Dundee, this continuing challenge to remember the sacrifices has been met through the Combined Services Association and SSAFA (soldiers, sailors, airmen and families association) of which I am Patron, and these Associations are led by the wonderful people who have kept our military heritage alive through the years.

I speak of course of Victor Herd, Chairman of the Combined Services, Bruce Kelly Secretary, and Willie Barr who keeps everyone on their toes, including myself of course. It was as Lord Provost and my passion for the Armed Forces that I started to work with them and the Combined Services in the interests of the City and beyond. In conjunction with all these efforts, of course was SSAFA Dundee & Angus Branch and the work within the Support Group which comprises Chairman Victor Herd, Secretary Bruce Kelly, two Veterans Frank Smith and Bill Naismith, Betty Wood of Whitehall Theatre fame, Mary Robertson of Asda who are one of our major sponsors that exist throughout the City. Last but not least Margaret Mather of Dundee Junior Showtime fame who is the Producer/Director of our major fund raising event the SSAFA Concert in the Caird Hall every year.

It has to be said of course that Margaret and the late Ronnie Coburn were the inspiration behind the Concert, firstly as the Help for Heroes Concert which was in existence first and then changed to SSAFA because of the need to operate locally and to make sure that all Service men and Woman and their families in all the conflicts of war, in all the places across the globe, would benefit through the generosity of the people of Dundee and Angus.

"I can't leave the Black Watch story without reminding everyone of the visit of myself, the Provosts of Perth & Kinross, Angus, and Fife, along with the top brass of the Black Watch Association went to 10 Downing Street to persuade the Prime Minister not to disband the proud history and name of the Black Watch, but we were referred to the Ministry of Defence and Secretary Jeff Hoon, who although polite and courteous was unmoved by our request".

BOATYAIRD

I served my time as an apprentice Marine Coppersmith in Dundee's Caledon Shipyard always referred to as the Boatyaird and it was a proud day that I first started there. Dundee had a long tradition of shipbuilding, and for innovation. The whaling industry in Dundee relied on the shipbuilders to supply vessels that could compete with other fleets, and when Dundee's shipbuilders began to put steam engines into these boats Dundee had a great advantage over others. So it was in the "boatyaird", with it's great sense of tradition and history that I began my time, and if any of your mates asked where you were working, you were sure to impress them when the Caledon was mentioned. Mind you signing up as a Coppersmith was not my intention, but I was 'talked' or duped into it by the gaffer of that shop Tam McDonald and as I have always accepted fate, I'm happy that he persuaded me that a Marine Coppersmith's life was the one for me.

The Caledon Shipyard was without doubt the most enjoyable time in my working life and it shaped and influenced my life time membership of the Union, the Dundee Labour Party and my venture into politics for some 40 years. Much has been said and written about the militancy of the Unions and how they were partly responsible for the demise of shipbuilding in the UK and here in Dundee there were practices that did not help, demarcation was a major reason and caused untold damage with relationships between Unions and the reasoning for some of the strikes left a lot to be desired and I can remember vividly one morning when the "yard electrician" whose job it was to "throw" the main switch that provided power for the Yard was late for work and one of the Managers did it for him, only to hear the dreaded call "everybody out" and of course every one lost a days wages, so what was the sense of that. I was involved in a potential stoppage myself when I used my initiative by removing an electricians cable tray a foot long so I could access my small copper piping, the result of that was that I was severly reprimanded by both the Unions and Management and these crazy practices carried on for years until a wee man called Tom Parnell arrived on the scene to sort it all out, but it was too little and too late by then and the fact that ships could be built quicker and cheaper abroad was the death knell of British Shipbuilding.

It was as I said earlier a great place to work and the comradeship, humour and banter of some of the BoatYaird characters or Dundee Worthies as they were called was a joy to behold and I remember for example, the formidable Gaffer Poe Tamson who ruled with a rod of iron and woe betide anyone who stepped out of line and I was there on the day when he caught a couple of stagers having an unofficial tea break with their tea cans and pies sitting on the staging ready to be demolished and Poe bellowed "whas pehs are they" and following the understandably silence he proceeded to eat the pies and drink out of one of the cans saying "they must be mine then" I have to say however many, many workers would get their own back on Mr Tamson during the evening stoppage and the legendary "Boatyaid Stampede" ie there was no clocking out system in the Yaird and every one had a brass check which they were given in the morning and at stoppage time would throw them into the boxes on the open gates and that's when it was too good an opportunity to miss with Poe supervising the exit gate and hundreds of checks reigning down on him, his language as you would expect as we bade him farewell was absolutely disgraceful. Poe Tamson of course was only one of the legendary characters that created the folklore that was the Boatyaird and made it an unforgettable place to ply your trade and others that come to mind like Wullie the Moth a welder who was attracted to the temporary light bulbs hanging throughout the which kept his hands warm, then there was Wee Davie who looked after the toilets and timed your visit, reporting to the Managers one day, that someone had been in for over 1 hour only to find that some prankster had put a pair of boots and braces behind a locked door and climbed over the top and left, there were other Worthies like Willie the Bat, Davie the Angry Cat, Billy Flatgloves and Wullie the Mouse. My good friend Davy Falconer MBE a welder who served his time with me, reminded me of the funeral of Wullie the Mouse in the "Crem" like all Boatyaid funerals was at 10.30am so everyone could get to the pub for opening time! and he also told me, that the Gate Keeper Jimmy Brownlee ex goalkeeper was the official Mourner at all the "send offs" When I recall the story about Wee Davie and toilets it reminds me of one of the two most embarrassing moments of my life, one at the boiler shop, just up the road from the Yard on an overtime night entering the no doors toilets at the Jetty,

Sitting on the wooden seat in total darkness, , when the Leerie came in singing a mournful song, kneeled down in front of me, proceeded to fill up his lanterns, engaging in a wee chat with a Marine Coppersmith who really did not want to indulge in conversation but had no means of escape. The other occasion funnaly enough was toilet related and involved myself and the Yard female cleaners, so for those who have never worked on the early days of a ship can I tell you it is unrealistic to leave the ship for a wee so the open deck becomes your refuge and if you can imagine the scene of this young 17 year old relieving himself with his back to the gangway, hearing the laughter of half a dozen females arriving on deck, turns round desperately trying to make himself decent, and the Leader of the Pack to a chorus of wolverines shouts "Dinna bather hidin that son, ehv seen plenty o them" well I never!

In looking back through the mists of time one day with good friend Davy Falconer we not only remembered all these Dundee worthies in the yard, we recalled other "practices" in the Boatyaid that have stayed with us for over 50 years, like Gordy Berry and all his red laders. If you had bairns and NHS dried milk tins you were in big demand because the red laders would sell you a tin of paint for half a crown which was great but the down side was that every Caledon workers house in the town was battleship grey! And the other problem on the ship was that you had to be on the move when they were around, as their motto was, if it doesn't move paint it, and the welders were no different, if you stayed in the one spot where they were working too long you could expect your steel toe capped boots to be welded to the metal decks. The acquisition of the "household paint" strange to say was never considered as theft, nor was the stripping of cables to get at the copper wire which like some of our copper pipes made its way to the scrappie. I would not like you to think that in all this mayhem no ships were built, on the contrary, our wonderful ships were made to last and our finishing trades were the best in the country and we did not do too badly for Boatyaid boys either as Davy Falconer and myself, were awarded MBE's and the father of Tam Wilson, my civic chauffeur, when Lord Provost was awarded the British Empire Medal for services to British Shipbuilding.

After my time was up, and I was a time- served man ready to earn a man's wage for a man's work, I was put on to a wage of £5 per week. You can imagine how chuffed I was getting this first weeks wages, but ironically it was also the last week's wages that I would earn as a Marine Coppersmith for quite a while, because I was called up that same week for National Service. This was in 1956 and my call up papers told me I had to attend the Caird Hall, along with many others, for a medical. National Service was compulsory for men in Britain in the 1950's so I was just being asked to do what all eligible young men were. I was quite excited, and thought I had nothing else to do than join my beloved Black Watch. I thought wrong. I was told in no uncertain terms that my National Service would be served with the Royal Air Force, and it was explained that it was in this arm of the services where I could best put to use my sheet-metal and coppersmiths skills. But although my dreams of an association with the Black Watch were punctured, I would get an opportunity much later in life to get seriously involved with this greatest of regiments, but you will have to wait until a little bit later in this book to read about the detail.

THE UNIONS

I cannot leave the Boatyaid without giving it the credit for my lifelong passion I have for the Union Movement which has I suppose influenced my way of thinking in most things I did throughout my life but having said that it would be untrue to say I agreed with everything the Unions did particularly by those who would try to use the Unions for their own agenda and for the objectives of the Labour Party and I speak of course of the Union Barons in the days when they used the block vote for their own interests and did not consult the Membership.

I joined the Union in the Boatyaid when I was only 17 years of age which represents 64 years unbroken membership but even in that first week when I received the Wee Red Book I complained about having part of my dues going to the Labour Party without being given the opportunity to either opt In or opt out, so it has taken 63 years and ex Labour Leader Ed Millaband to get the message but I have to say only because of the chaos and bad publicity that transpired through Unite and the selection of Labour Candidates in Falkirk. I came to terms with that form of bullying of course because at the time I was not aware of anyone who was not a member of a Union in the Yard and in any case I was to become a Union activist, a Labour Party Member, a Chair of the local Labour Party, a Ward Councillor on both Tayside Regional Council, Dundee City Council, and finally Lord Provost and Lord Lieutenant of the City of Dundee.

As an employee and Union Member in the Shipyard I grew up with the mentality and madness of strike after strike but it was not until some years later that I came to realise the futility of stoppages that seemed to have no rhyme or reason, but having said that, there were occasions when our last line of defence was justifiable and the 13 week Apprentices strike in the early fifties which I was part of springs to mind. I became a Shop Steward in the Yard and elsewhere in my working life and a factory Convenor in a manufacturing Plant called Nasbrit in Gourdie Industrial Estate where I led a seven week strike in support of the lower paid workers. I remember the support given to us by "comrades" from Timex and NCR and others which was described as secondary picketing and although I was grateful at the time, I agreed with the dreaded Margaret Thatcher when she made secondary picketing illegal, well why not, why should good employers be punished by their own well looked after employees when they were off work supporting others. Our stoppage was successful in the sense that the lower paid were upgraded but seven weeks without pay was difficult for everyone and one Toolmaker sold his house and went back to England. I think I was blacklisted by the Company and they said there would have to be redundancies because of the strike so I offered to leave if my son John, who had not been there long, was kept in a job. The deal was done and I left but unknown to them I had a job lined up so it was smiles all round and everyone was happy. John was unaware of all this however and will know for the first time if he reads this, sorry son.

It would be true to say that at that time many of the union members throughout the country were concerned, not only about the total disregard the union barrons had for the memberships wishes, by invoking the block vote procedure, but also regarding the negative image that was being perceived by the public as a whole. We were unfortunetly, unable to do anything about it, but help came from a very unlikely source in the shape of the Prime Minister of the day, Margaret Thatcher who being a very determined lady sought confrontation with the Union Barons on secondary picketing and the Block Votes which she won of course. I must have had a rush of blood because I contacted the Evening Telegraph praising the Iron Lady and calling the Union Barons dinosaurs! This was to come back and haunt me at the following local elections when a good friend Terry McMahon confronted me about my Telly article and my love for Margaret Thatcher, not quite true of course, the love bit, but to deny that she had no admirable qualities would be very churlish. I am sure that my determination to speak my mind did not affect Terry's, or others support for me, as I never lost an election throughout my political career. I continued to operate as a shop steward in most of the Organisations I worked with, but Management was beckoning when I moved to Cape Asbestos at the Carolina Power Station on the Waterfront, Longannet near Edinburgh and finally joined Community Industry as the Deputy to legendary Chic Farquhar who I succeeded as the Training Manager for Dundee, Aberdeen Fife and Stirling. I obtained a City and Guilds Diploma in Management whilst there and a Member of the Chartered Institute in Personnel followed, which was to stand me in good stead when I became the Convenor of Personell on Dundee City Council which was to involve me in the fractured relationship between the legendary Bruce Kelly, Council Administrator and the Lord Provost of the day Councillor Helen Wright.

BRUCE KELLY REPORT

The fractured relationship that I speak of between the then Lord Provost Helen Wright and the Council Administrator Bruce Kelly was brought to my attention in my capacity of Personnel Convener on the 28th of September 1999 by the Director of the Personnel Department and Lord Provost Helen Wright. This was of course extremely bad news and worse was to follow because a press release was imminent indicating that the altercation between Mr Kelly and the Lord Provost had happened 4 weeks previously. As personnel Convener on behalf of the Council and its elected members I found this unacceptable and with permission of my colleagues and the Chief Whip Councillor Chic Farquhar conducted my own investigation and reported back to the Labour Group and the Labour Party.

The Investigation Report is factual and was not disputed by anyone at the time and I am not sure how many copies remain, but if I was a betting man I would say my original may be the only one as it was quite embarrassing to many people, so because it contains text and reconciliations of job descriptions I am presenting it to you in a readable form, with the proviso that it is available for anyone who would wish to scrutinise it.

My Investigation and discussions with Staff

On the 27th August 1999 Bruce Kelly was asked to attend the Chief Executive office where he was offered to take early retirement and declined. He was also offered redeployment but it was suggested that he may not like the post but to take a week's leave and think about it. When I asked the Chief Executive if this was an accurate account he agreed, but denied Mr Kelly's allegation the the Lord Provost said she would not work with him again and he could not return to the Council Chambers, I did ask if Mr Kelly could have taken their conversation to mean just that he said it was possible.

Meetings between the CEO, Councillor Sturrock, Chief Whip Chic Farquhar, Councillor Merv Rolf and myself followed and in response to my question of why it had not been a personnel issue on the 27th August, the CEO indicated he wished to handle it himself.

A Review of the Council Chambers procedures and staff duties was instigated with a view to making changes and this Review commenced on 9th September 1999-13 days after the CEO and Mr Kelly met and this Review continued whilst Mr Kelly was off work.

The Review

I attended a Meeting with a member of the Personnel Department, and the Director and I asked for clarification on Meetings on the 10th September1999 when Bruce Kelly's job description was discussed and was there an assumption that Mr Kelly would not return to work? On the 17th September Council Officer Frank Traynor's Job Description was verified by Council Officer Bill Whytock whilst his immediate Supervisor Mr Kelly was still off work. Was this another indication that Mr Kelly would not be allowed to return to work in the Chambers, and on the 24th September the completed new job descriptions were presented to the Director of Personnel.

(4 days before I was told what was going on) and in response to my question of how many job descriptions were changed the answer was only Mr Kelly's with only 2 changes.

Following the above Review I requested all the new job descriptions and made comparisons with the present job descriptions and found that the present Council Administrator Mr Bruce Kelly's job description and the new one with a change of name to Council Co-ordinator contained 2 minor changes

(1) collate information and prepare reports and speeches for the Lord Provost or Depute as requested and

(2) administer the Lord Provost Charity Fund (none of the two of them realistic).

I concluded the Review process was flawed, that Bruce Kelly was being unfairly treated, and the Review process was designed to remove him. I conveyed these findings to the Director of Personnel and he agreed to abort the Review.

At further meetings I asked the Chief Executive and Director of Personnel if there was any basis or reason why Mr Kelly should be removed from his post, i.e. was there any disciplinary procedures ever taken against him and was there anything of a disciplinary nature on his record. The answer to my questions on more than one occasion was no and this further reinforced my view that Bruce Kelly had been treated unfairly.

At the various meetings that took place I described the official procedures to be used when it was thought that a member of staff was not performing his/her work duties as is required. Simply, that the member of staff should be interviewed and then given the opportunity to improve his/her performance over a stated period of time. The Director of Personnel agreed that this was, and is, the proper procedure laid down and confirmed to me that this procedure was not adopted for Bruce Kelly. I therefore concluded once again that Bruce Kelly had no case to answer as this was another indication that he had been treated unfairly.

I conveyed my view and my findings to Council Leader, Councillor Julie Sturrock and because of non-agreement on this issue I indicated that if Mr Bruce Kelly was not allowed to return to his same job then I would resign. I conveyed this decision to senior members of the Labour Group and the Labour Party.

Mr Kelly returned to his work but there were difficulties and there was a view that he was not being allowed to carry out his work and although I could not testify to the level of that, I could testify that I witnessed him being completely ignored by the Lord Provost at programme meetings in preference to Council Officer Bill Whytock with whom she conducted all her business.

Mr Kelly I think had had enough and eventually retired.

The story did not end there of course and Mr Kelly was duly nominated for Citizen of the Year and the Lord Provost approached myself and Chic Farquhar with concerns that if Bruce Kelly was selected it would cause her great embarrassment. We pointed out that Bruce was entitled to be nominated like anyone else but she disagreed and said she would see the Chief Executive. Chic later informed me that Helen had told him that Alex Stephen, David Dorward, and Patricia McIlquham would join the Panel with voting rights, but Mr Stephen was the only one of the three who took part.

Criteria was introduced at the selection meeting which excluded Bruce Kelly and others, one of the criteria introduced was that an activity nominated for, which was carried out during employment excluded the candidate. I indicated that three former Citizens of the Year had achieved their honour through their employment but I was informed by the Chief Executive that this would not happen again. I was quite rightly of the opinion that Bruce Kelly's nomination was discussed at Officer Level and because the Lord Provost lobbied the Chief Executive, myself and Councillor Farquhar the whole process was tainted.

Bruce Kelly

At any other time I might have supported the view of the Chief Executive for whom I had great respect, but a great Dundonian and a great Ambassador for the City of Dundee was denied a possible, deserved recognition, from a grateful City and denied a fond farewell as he left the City Chambers, in many ways his Chambers.

LORD PROVOST HELEN WRIGHT

Following the unsatisfactory departure of Bruce Kelly from the City Chambers there was wide spread condemnation towards Lord Provost Wright and the Council that a man who had served ten Lord Provosts over a period of thirty years should be treated in this manner and not get the retiral he deserved. It was not long after this that the storm clouds began to gather, documents and expenses records of Mrs Wright were appearing in the press on an almost daily basis with an embarrassed labour group meeting on a regular basis to try and sort it out, without success I my add. The support for the Lord Provost was ebbing fast and members of the Group were not pleased when the Officers of the Council seemed to be getting the blame by Mrs Wright, and the claims for £2.00 for First Minister Donald Dewar's church funeral collection and the Anti-Poverty Forum was the last straw for all the members of the Group.

Mrs Wright was asked to resign on more than one occasion but refused and the SNP requested a meeting of the City Council to lodge a vote of no confidence and this meeting took place on the 30th March. It is the custom for all political groups to meet before a Council meeting to discuss the Agenda items and prepare a strategy for the business at hand and this duly happened. There was no support for the Lord Provost at that meeting and it was likely that a decision to abstain would have been made, were it not for the intervention of the Secretary of the local labour party, as he said, on behalf of the Executive. The Secretary of the local labour party asked to join that evenings meeting and told us that the Executive were instructing us to support Councillor Wright and vote accordingly that evening, and if not prepared to do that, then our membership cards would be withdrawn, and the group, many of them long standing members were not prepared to make that sacrifice and had no option but to concede and vote for the Lord Provost. It was not enough as it turned out to carry the amendment on the vote and the Lord Provost was removed from Office.

Following these events Councillor Wright complained to the Labour Party, citing seventeen allegations against the labour group, and we were interviewed on an individual basis, but not one of the allegations or complaints was upheld.

Much was written at the time of Councillor Wrights allegations of a conspiracy but there was no hint of a conspiracy at the time and no evidence to support that claim. The fact of the matter was that a majority of councillors, out with the Labour Group democratically voted against the Lord Provost, but it would be naive to think that senior politicians on the Council who cared for the reputation of the City and the Council were not talking to each other and were determined to restore moral and move forward, but they would have done that on an individual basis through their own political party, but let's not forget that without the blackmail tactics of the labour party it was likely that not a single Councillor would have supported Mrs Wright that evening. We will never know of course but In many ways it was a tragic affair and in my opinion a disaster for woman in general, in that Dundee being a "She" City and having waited all those years to elect a woman as Lord Provost, would have to face a situation that would set back their just cause for many years. Let's hope that sometime soon, that will be addressed and we will have a female once more as the Civic Head of the City.

At this time Helen was quoted in the press as saying that it was all a misunderstanding and this may or may not be the case, but what is undeniable is that in refusing to resign, against all the predictable pressures put on her, she never once faltered in her determination to stay in Office, and her raw courage was quite remarkable.

TAYSIDE REGIONAL COUNCIL AND TAYSIDE CONTRACTS

Regional councils and district councils were abolished under the Local Government (Scotland) Act in 1994 and replaced by a single-tier local government structure in 19996. Tayside Regional Council, of which I was a Ward Councillor, was replaced by the unitary councils of Dundee, Angus, and Perth & Kinross and although I was for a short time a Councillor on the Region I welcomed the opportunity to become a Councillor for the City of Dundee.

I did enjoy my time as a Regional Councillor and I have to confess it was quite exciting even though Labour was in opposition with the SNP having taken control at the last election of that authority. With all due respect I have to say that the calibre of that SNP administration did not match the expertise of the present and first SNP administration of Dundee City Council. We had very senior councillors in that Labour Group who had the experience to exploit the weaknesses of an SNP group who were all over the place at times and disagreed, sometimes more times with each other, than they did with us.

We were able to work out would you believe, the commitments time wise, that some of their members had and the serious problem it gave them if we had to have late meetings, so the records will tell of the many meetings we ensured carried on in to the early hours of the morning. Their desperation to get home resulted in early concessions to us, and it looked at times they were the opposition.

They made many political mistakes of course that were fatal for them and the "electric light bulb for everyone springs to mind as does the £10 giveaway that was declared illegal by the Chief Executive and of course their disastrous decision to pay off all the cleaners. We capitalised in all of that and a good time was had by all. There is a myth within the general public that we are all enemies, as different political groups, but that is not true, when the slagging stops we get on fine and there may be some truth, that we all fight amongst ourselves more than we do with our opponents, sounds familiar!

When the reorganisation of the regional and district councils took place and Dundee, Angus, and Perth & Kinross became unitary councils the split up of departments and finances caused some conflict, and I am sure Dundee lost out financially to the tune of some millions of pounds, and what we had to do to protect the jobs and livelihoods of Tayside Contracts who were the building and trunk roads operations of Tayside Regional Council, was for Dundee, Angus and Perth & Kinross to become 3 constituent authorities responsible for the operations of Tayside Contracts. This we did very successfully and that leads me to my part in all of that.

The Convenorship of Tayside Contracts in a political sense consisted of the Convenor and 2 vice-convenors with all three rotating the convenorship and it was whilst I was the Convenor there were circumstances that were to change my life forever culminating in myself being thrown out of the Scottish Parliament!

The tender for the trunk roads, which had been previously been granted to local authorities, came up for renewal and the local authorities lost out to a recently created business BEAR (Amy in England) who had no staff, no equipment and no locations to work from, and undercut the local authorities by millions of pounds. This cynical exercise resulted in Tayside Contracts having to sub-contract from BEAR to save the jobs and livelihoods of their workers. Every local authority decided to attend the Scottish Parliament where the issue was to be debated and have a silent protest. Yours truly must have forgot that plan, because when a liberal politician asked the then Transport Minister Sarah Boyak to explain her thinking her very bland reply enraged me, and I was on my feet shouting, yes shouting, you are a disgrace to the Labour Party, and I will remember for ever The Presiding Officer David Steel of the Scottish Parliament saying "remove that man from the Chamber" I was of course "helped out" by two burly messengers at arms and every local authority walked out in support. The rest is history, I spent the next few hours in Deacon Brodie's with orange juice coming out of my ears, reporters calling, overtures from the television media, and there was even a suggestion of a shirt being printed with Che' Letford on it instead of Che' Gavera the notorious revolutionary. A heady experience I can tell you, all because I had an unrehearsed rush of blood to the head.

I have to tell you however that, that rush of blood was to indirectly set me on a collision course with my colleagues in the Labour Group, the Labour Party and put my membership of the Labour Party in jeopardy, so let me explain. The decision taken by the Minister Sarah Boyak to award the Trunk Roads Contract to a private company did not go down well with local authorities, the workforce, the unions and the general public as a whole, and it was the intention of our group leader at the time Ian Luke to put a motion to Council of " no confidence" in Sarah Boyak which most people would have supported, myself in particular, but the Party got wind of it and decreed that we could not do that against a Labour Party Minister. I warned them that if we did not do that first, the SNP would certainly put a motion forward and if they did I would have in all conscience to support it. All hell broke loose and I was warned by colleagues that if I went down this path I would be finished as a labour party councillor. The SNP as I predicted put forward their motion of no confidence and I asked for a recess and we adjourned in to the Twinning Room and I told them of my intentions. It was an extremely long discussion of maybe thirty minutes and advice of, go home, go to the toilet which all went unheeded and I returned to the Chambers and voted with the SNP. That action was raised by a councillor colleague at our very large General Meeting of the Labour Party and he got no support what so ever which tells you a lot about what everyone felt about Sarah Boyak. The thing for readers to remember in all of this is that I supported the SNP for the first time, long, long, before I became Lord Provost

All of these circumstances I was involved in were driven by a desire to protect the jobs of those people throughout the region and most important the people of Dundee and my union background, being the Convenor and indeed being the Personnel Convenor for Dundee City Council, meant that I always had the interests of staff first and foremost in my mind.

That desire to see fair play for staff, and with regard to Tayside Contracts, was to invite controversy and end up being reported to the Standards Commission on a charge of breaching my code of conduct.

As one of two Vice-Convenors (Constituent Authorities Convenor-ship is rotated on a yearly basis) I attended a pre-agenda Joint Committee meeting to determine the acceptance of an agenda for a forthcoming Tayside Contracts Joint Committee meeting. Those attending that meeting were the then Convenor, myself, the other Vice-Convenor, Depute Chief Executive Finance Dundee City Council as the "Proper Officer" Depute Chief Executive Support Services Dundee City Council as Clerk and the Managing Director of Tayside Contracts.

Prior to the start of the meeting I indicated I needed the relevant papers and the Managing Director gave me his own, having spare papers with him. There was disagreement with the contents of the papers regarding the level of regrading salary for the Head of Personnel which in my opinion and others placed the salary increase at an excessive level and out of all proportion to the levels of salary levels given to other staff in Tayside Contracts and the other three constituent Local Authorities. (It is worth mentioning at this time that the proposed increase was £9,000.)

In leaving that situation for the moment, it is important to mention that there was a contentious correspondence issue within the business papers, concerning the Head of Personnel of Tayside Contracts requesting a regrading which amounted to a pay rise of nine thousand pounds per year to give her parity with her colleagues

I was not agreeable to this outrageous demand and voiced my disapproval and the issue was to be returned to at a later time. It was the next day when the chief whip and I came across an email in the papers given to me the previous day and I am sure when that person realised where it was he must have died a thousand deaths.

The contents of the email revealed that the Head of Personnel, making the regrading claim had sent it to the Managing Director of Tayside Contracts who would obviously be making the recommendation to the Board whether to approve it or not. This in itself was a breach of the code of conduct but the contents went far beyond what was acceptable in industrial relations and more important a lack of fair play.

The email itself sent to and received by the Managing Director criticised the Director of Finance of Dundee City Council, and the Director of Legal for not supporting her claim and worse still as far as I was concerned was her request to her "Boss" that " Ron (the Convenor) should try and persuade John(myself) to see the merits of her claim" and in addition to these outrageous comments someone called Frank according to the email, was enlisted to find out what salary the Director of Personnel of Dundee District Council was receiving. You have to consider that this unsavoury request was being put forward by a person who would as the head of human relations be making decisions on the pay conditions of the workforce and would certainly not be agreeing to thousands of pounds per year in one quantum leap for her own staff.

I reported this to the Convenor, who I am sure discussed it with his political colleagues, and he said there would be no further discussions and he would be presenting the regrading document to the Tayside Contracts Joint Committee for approval.

I prepared a document and a motion for that Committee indicating that I wished the three Chief Executives of the three Constituent Authorities to meet and discuss all the circumstances surrounding the intended regrading issue and included with this paper the contentious email.

At the Board the Convenor took the unusual step of speaking to my agenda item before I had spoken to it, and indeed invited the Managing Director to do the same. This was a blatant disregard for procedure as the Managing Director is of course not an elected member.

The Depute Provost of Angus an SNP colleague of the Convenor proposed to go to the vote immediately, and I was prevented from speaking to my own motion!

I resigned from the Board with immediate effect, and not "being born yesterday" realised that the SNP Councillors had "stitched me up" It has to be said however that none of my own colleagues supported my course of action and it was not until sometime later that the Conservative Councillor Neil Powrie said they should all have walked out, too little and too late of course. I knew that the contentious email was going to be buried and never see the light of day so I went to the Press and made it public

The Head of Personal reported me to the Standards Commission for Scotland claiming I had broken my code of conduct, all parties concerned were interviewed, myself included, and the short version is that I was cleared of all wrong doing, and the pleasing result was that the lady in question, in addition to being unsuccessful in her complaint against me, and if my memory serves me well I am sure did not get her exorbitant claim and she is no longer with the company.

It may well be, that embarking on that journey of trying to right a wrong, I bit off more than I could chew, but there is a great saying is there not "you can lose the battle as long as you don't lose the war" Well let's face it, I was the one who was exonerated by the Standards Commission and "they" were the ones who were criticised and lost their credibility, so bad judgement I am afraid ladies and gentleman, you will just have to live with it won't you.

GUILDRY

In my long tenure of Office as Lord Provost I had the great privilege to work with, and be supported by the historical institutions of our City including the Guildry, the Nine Trades, and the three Trades. The Rotary does not have the historical significance of those mentioned but they do share a similarity as far as business, commerce, and Merchants are concerned and other than the three Trades I am a proud Member of the other Organisations mentioned.

In dealing with the Guildry first it would be true to say their history goes back further than the others and although they all have their own identity there is a bond that exists between them and many Members are intertwined with each other.

The origins of the Guildry Incorporation of Dundee can be traced back to the 12th century through being a Royal Burgh, when the influence of the Burgesses gave them a monopoly of trade granted to them by Charter, from Robert the 1st and his Charter of 1327. The Guildry was founded basically as a Society of Merchants, meeting together to defend their own interests, however the Guildry's authority was exercised over anyone, male or female who tried to make a living by opening a shop until the nineteenth century, and those who would not or could not, for financial reasons enter the Incorporation, were compelled to pay a licence or face court action.

The abolition of all the privileges took place in 1846 and although there was a misconception, held at the present day I may add, that women were not eligible to join the Incorporation, is simply not true, but what is true is that the introduction of women being eligible is shrouded in the folklore of the Guildry and to be honest their story is quite amazing.

In 1818 the "Collector" as he was called and the person who controlled the purse strings of the Guildry Incorporation reported that several shops had opened in the Wellgate and he was instructed to contact them all by letter, telling them that they must all pay dues to continue trading and avoid prosecution. The unusual feature of this communication was that the letters were sent out with the misapprehension that all the recipients were male, but lo and behold, several of them were women who with great haste paid their dues and were registered.
The die was cast, the rest is history, and it is not known what became of the Controller who committed the cardinal sin of not checking the gender of the shopkeepers, who being women were not at that time eligible to become Burgesses and Merchants of the City.

The Burgesses of course played a major role in the development and history of our great City and the request to me from the Guildry, and Innes Duffis in particular, to attempt to resurrect this great Institution and take it forward as a Charitable Organisation was to set me on a collision course once more with the Labour Group with the exception of Councillor Joe Morrow.

The removal of privileges for the Burgesses in 1846 did not prevent me as Lord Provost from attempting to resurrect the Burgess Ticket, the people who had made the request were the same people whose commitment over the years to the City, and the Council I hasten to add, is quite magnificent, and It is right and proper as the former Lord Provost that I pay tribute to the Guildry, the Nine Trades, the Three Trades and indeed Rotary, for their generosity and thousands of pounds donated to the Lord Provost Charity Fund which along with other donations including the Lord Provost Charity Ball, paid for youth trips abroad, Christmas Lunches in the City Chambers, funding for youth organisations, needy people and particularly disadvantaged kids at Christmas time, so if our Tax Payers worry that their taxes are paying for these very commendable events rest assured that is not the case, it is the generosity of the people of Dundee and the Organisations I have just mentioned who make it possible and they deserve our grateful thanks.

The request to reinstate the Burgesses came from the Archivist to The Nine Incorporated Trades Innis Duffus who tells us, in one of his many fine books, that it was not easy to become a Burgess, money, authority and influence seemed to be the order of the day with a system at that time that was described as "perpetuating and as corrupt as the Council". I asked Innis to outline his Project and present me with a document that I could present in the first instance to the Leader of the Administration and thereafter the Labour Group before going to full Council.

The document given to me had no representation of woman members and this was of course unacceptable to myself and the Leader of the Administration so Innis had to amend the document accordingly. I insisted that the makeup of any Burgess Committee would have to have three woman, three men and chaired by the Lord Provost and in that form it was presented to the Labour Group for their consideration. It was met with little enthusiasm and only Councillor Joe Morrow was prepared to support me in something I thought would be good for the City considering it was intended to be a charitable organisation. It was extremely difficult, indeed impossible, to get the agreement of the Group, the Leader suggested we leave it until after the election and look at it again, but never did. The truth will out, as they say and a very senior member of the Group who was later to become Leader voiced the opinion and the underlying reason why we should not agree the request. Why, he said, should we support the wishes of business people who "do not vote for us anyway"

This was a disgraceful statement of course which angered myself and Councillor Morrow who said that was a terrible message to send out to the people of the City and the business community and it was quite ludicrous to suggest that all business people voted other than labour. It was never taken forward by a Labour Administration, but after what seemed an eternity it went through Council, all be it reluctantly, by an SNP Administration and flourishes to this day. I am sure Innes was not happy with me personally at my failure to achieve success quicker than I did but politics always gets in the way of progress!

There was, of course, many positives for me personally in the resurrection of the Burgesses all these years ago, I was installed as "The First Burgess" at the time, and recently I have been invited by the Trustees to join the Prganisation, and it will give great pleasure working with friends, old and new, as we take this wonderful and historical Instution of our city forward.

I am also grateful to the Guildry of course for their parting gift to me when I retired, in the shape of the wooden bench in the City Square which bears my name. I can very easily now say to those who sit on it "you are in my chair" and when they say "how, is your name on it" I can then say that it is, but I think I will pass on that one.

SPORT

In looking back over the years and remembering what was important in my life it is hard to deny that my involvement and time in football was high on the list in what I achieved and together with being the Lord Provost were the ones I would like to be remembered for.

Starting at the beginning takes me back to Butterburn Boys Club, the kingpins at that time, and Club Leader Baxter Mitchell and assistant Dave McHardy who years later was to join me at St Columba BC. I remember the pretty basic training methods we had at Butterburn compared to the training portfolio which I was fortunate to get from my old and present friend Jim McLean which I used when I managed St Columba. I did not as you would imagine, adopt the Butterburn philosophy of changing into shorts and sannies at the Graham Street hut and going out running for an hour, whilst Baxter and Dave were still in the hut. That was maybe more than what other teams did because Butterburn won everything in sight at that time.

I moved on to another team called Victoria Boys and remember the Manager Jim Headridge who used to call me Gabby the Goalie and one of my team mates was the "wee man" Jimmy Reid who played for Dundee United and had his shop in Seagate. Jimmy was a good friend of mine and used to supply me with Bingo items for my youth club at a very reasonable price but every time he met me he always said "did you ever give me that fiver you owed me" a nice man indeed with a great sense of humour and a great footballer.

Whilst working in the Caledon Shipyard I played for Craigmore who were in the Angus Amateur League and at 17 years of age was the youngest player they had, the team being full of ex Junior League players and I was myself beginning to be noticed by the Juniors and had a small bit in the local newspaper (I think it was the Tully) that Hibs were watching me. That didn't come to anything but the Caledon Engineers team officials approached me saying that a Junior side were going to sign me and if I signed for them first they would get a small donation for their club, so I signed the form, never played for them, but I did play for both Broty Athletic and Downfield Junior Clubs. I started to court a young lady called Betty Grant, eventually married her and that was the end of my footballing career, and I suppose I was a little too short in the bum to be a professional goalkeeper anyway but they didn't call me "The Cat" for nothing.

I did have a wee mishap injury wise whilst playing for Craigmore when I dived at the feet of a young man, I remember his name would you believe, Ian Strachan, who accidentally of course, broke my jaw in an argument with his knee, hospital followed, jaws wired with silver plated gum shields for a couple of months I think, lost a stone in weight because I could only take liquids and know what, I continued to play, without the Docs permission of course. I continued to play football when I went to the RAF and National Service but only for the Station Team, I did try my hand at cricket whilst in the RAF or to be more precise I tried my face! I thought wicketkeeper was the ideal position for me but the first ball came up and hit me in the face, down like a sack of tatties and out like a light, a one ball wonder, never to be seen again, but I was to be seen in the football team and would you believe in the Station Boxing Team!

Boxing

I enjoyed my two years in the Royal Air Force which was made easier for me because I was a member of an elite team of sheet metal workers who worked specifically on the V Bombers and the Canberra Bombers, but being in the Football Team and the Boxing Team gave you special privileges, particularly our own meal table which meant no queuing up and looking for a seat so my so called mates who put my name on the entry list for Boxing did me a big favour. The worst part of the training was the Padre who had homicidal tendencies and put you together with a sparring partner who was sometimes a couple of stone heavier and you would get knocked about a bit with the Padre shouting " get in there you cissy" At lightweight however I was unbeaten and was entered for the Bomber Command Championships at RAF Hemswell in Lincolnshire and amazing would you believe I fought a Dundee lad called Willie Dryden in the semi-final and beat him, my joy was short lived however because I was posted to Germany the next day and had all the requisite injections, only for a change of plan for me to stay in England but because I had been given the needles I was excluded and yes you have guessed it Willie Dryden the semi-finalist was drafted in and duly won the Championship. I have always claimed since, that I was hypothetically the Lightweight Champion of Bomber Command so if you are reading this Willie - I want my Trophy.

I returned from the RAF in 1958 and decided to take up a career in refereeing within the Scottish Football Referees Association (SFRA) and continued with them until 1965 when I entered the youth football arena. I have to say I enjoyed my time being a referee but like everyone else I had a very unpleasant baptism as a novice referee and one I will remember for ever! The game in question and my first was Monifieth Tayside versus Grays United in the Midlands Amateur League with the final score 6-5 and the game and I was absolutely horrendous. The most difficult part of the game for me, remembering there was no linesman, was at the turn around after half time I did not have a clue trying to remember which way each side was playing and gave some dodgy thrown in decisions to a torrent of abuse from each side, I decided to play it cute and would shout either "blue ball" or "red ball" depending which colours they were playing in and that got me through the game which as I remember ended with a bit of a melee and a ludicrous statement from the winners that I had a good game, you have to laugh don't you. I did improve of course and enjoyed the experience, especially if you had a good game and I think I became one of the best referees getting some important games in the process. There were two occasions that stayed with me always, the first was running the line in a Final of the North of the Tay Cup and being introduced to the Referee as one of the up and coming young referees and would the referee give some advice. The referee was the Scotland and EUFA whistler John Gordon who took me aside and said "John, when you go out there and see all these faces, you're right and they are all f......wrong, I took that advice and never looked back. The other occasion was quite amusing and involved one of my fellow novice referees who for this sorry tale I will call Billy. I worked for the National Cash Register (NCR) and they had a great team that actually won the Scottish Amateur Cup at Hampden, but they had a terrible reputation for playing offside, well Billy refereed their game against Condor from Arbroath and when he told me that NCR had been beaten 2-0 that game I was shocked and asked him what happened to them, to be told from Billy " ...well John, they really cheesed me off with their offside trap all the time so I let a couple of offside goals stand for Condor and that sorted them out! You won't be surprised to hear that Billy did not complete his training.

In looking back over the years I spent in sport particularly my first love football, firstly as a player and then a qualified referee another chapter in the book of my life was about to open and become a defining moment not only for me but for many of the young people in the City.

In 1965 my oldest son John, then 9 years of age returned one Friday evening from Charleston Primary School where he went every week for a kick about in the School gym run by a Mr David Maillie who was later to become my life long best friend. John told me Mr Maillie had asked all the boys to ask their Dads to come along the following Friday to give him a hand and John Senior was the only father to turn up.

Dave ran older boys called Charleston Boys who played in a Saturday league and asked me to take the younger kids and build a team and because he had a set of all green tops we called them Charleston Celtic which was great for him because he was a Celtic Supporter and not so good for me because I was a Rangers fan! Well we played friendly games with another local team called Charleston Athletic until we were sick of the sight of each and with the help of the other Manager Alex Baird we decided a year later to form The Sunday Boys League and invited others through the Press to join us. We assembled 8 teams, the names of which I remember all these many years ago, Charleston Celtic, Charleston Athletic, St. Pius, Macalpine, Fintry CC, Charleston Rangers, United Juniors, and Club Romano. In those days before the League was formed we just kicked the ball about on the Sundays on the existing pitches used on a Saturday, if the park ranger didn't chase us off. So, I decided to ask the Council if we could use them officially and asked for a meeting. The evening of the Parks Department meeting in the Chambers chaired by Councillor Chic Farquhar was bizarre to say the least and the actions of the Officials of the Associations of the Angus Amateurs, the Midlands Amateurs, and the Dundee District Juveniles was a disgrace. They all attended to express their opposition to granting us the football pitches on the basis Sunday football was banned by the SFA and the added complaint that were asking for the pitches free of charge. Chic Farquhar was our hero that evening as he agreed to both our requests and The Sunday Boys League was born and better still the first League Champions in 1967 was Charleston Celtic. We refereed our own games in the first year or two because the Refs were hogtied by the SFA as well, but when the Leagues expanded and we agreed to pay Refs expenses they came to their senses very quickly. The other momentous event as far as I was concerned was that Dave Maillie returned to the younger kids and because we had extra teams coming and Dave was never going to call his team Charleston Celtic "B", Dundee Celtic Boys was born which delighted my best friend and

Lochee United Clubhouse - the day I drew them as the Home Team in the Scottish Cup. Bette is at the front.

if I am honest it delighted me also, Dave now deceased and I were, as I said, lifelong friends definitely not like two peas in a pod but we both liked to win and on most occasions we usually did.

I was the Secretary and Match Secretary for the Sunday Boys League in the first four years of its existence and it was a wonderful experience and great privilege to be involved in its creation, and it gives me a sense of great pride to watch the kids on a Sunday knowing I had a hand in what they do. I have great admiration for what the present Officials have done to expand the League, now called The Dundee and District Youth Football Association and through their dedication over many years the young people of this City and beyond will realise their aspirations in this beautiful game of ours.

It was time to move on however and myself and Alex Baird of Charleston Athletic pooled our resources and made application to the Angus Amateur Association in the Saturday league, but lo and behold, there were echoes of the past through the skulduggery of the teams in the Angus

Lochee United and their "Home Game" draw - apopular man that day!

Amateurs who turned us down in the hope of getting all our young stars, and sure enough we were approached immediately after the meeting and asked to join by each Club. I met with Lochee Boys Club shortly after and they wanted me and the team, but not Alex Baird. I could not agree to that and Alex and I spoke to St Columba Boys Club and Billy Boyle Snr. The Meeting went well until the local Priest insisted that we could only play youngsters from the parish which went against everything I stood for and in addition we were bringing in a team of youngsters who were much sought after and most of them signed for Senior Clubs and some of them went on to play for Scotland. I made the point that I would decide who played for me and where the kid came from and whatever his religion, was irrelevant. I got up to leave, only to be stopped by Billy Boyle who agreed with my point of view and I never met that Priest again. The rest is history and St Columba Boys Club went on to years of success that was unparalleled in the history of youth football in the City and on the way becoming a nursery side for Dundee United and my new and everlasting friend in the shape of Jim McLean of Dundee United Football Club. My relationship with Jim was very special over the years and on occasions he gave me the privilege of sharing a dugout with him and one of his coaches Ian Campbell. Jim as you will all know had a fiery temper and I witnessed him in action on more than one occasion but it was quite bizarre on my part to quite enjoy the experience. In the 30 plus years

With Legend, Jim McLean at Tanadice. A wee smile - they must have scored!

friendship we enjoyed he never had a bad word to say to me but came very close one day when I must have had a rush of blood to the head and I said to him, "Jim why do you play Graeme (Payne) wide when he likes the middle of the park" and without a trace of a smile he told me "Mr Letford, you run your team and I will run mine" I got my own back another time when he told me that I thought the sun shone out of Graeme's behind (or words to that effect) "Well Jim when he played for me I never allowed him to wear his socks around his ankles, "get the tie ups on" and whilst I'm at it I did not let Davy Narey wear a headband either " Get that headband back in your bag David" I said. That particular team with David Narey, Graeme Payne and all the others, was considered the best ever youth team the City ever had but we had other fine teams and some other great players who carried on in the footsteps of these giants of the 60s and the 70s but when my good friend Colin Davidson who was my steadying influence and my co-worker, had a heart attack and died I lost some enthusiasm and when ironically, (considering my early days in Sunday football) my players wanted to play Sunday as well as Saturday, I called it a day and bowed out at the end of that season taking with me treasured memories that will be with me forever.

LABOUR PARTY AND RESIGNATION

"I have mentioned in some detail my deteriorating relationship with certain members of the Labour Party, and I say certain members, because it would be unfair and too broad a brush to include those who may share my views, but were not prepared to go down the path that I did and there will be those who will always be my friends, so those who continually undermined me over the years would be foolish to think I stood alone and would be surprised indeed to learn of the very senior members of the Labour Party who indicated their support to me and although I knew that they could not do that publicly I will never ever reveal their names, I was never the less grateful for their kind words.

I said at the beginning of my book that I would be honest and forthright and I will take the opportunity to do that now and let you the reader, whoever you may be, make your own judgement on the rights and wrongs regarding my resignation.

If my memory serves me well, my first altercation with the Labour Party was when I joined the Union in the Caledon Shipyard at 17 years of age and on receiving my "little red book" from the Union discovered that the rule book stated that unless I signed the attached page there would be a subscription charge that would go to the Labour Party. I objected to that (rebel at an early age) and said so to the Union about an outdated principal of contracting out instead of contracting in and it took 63 years and Ed Milliband to advocate scrapping a rule I never agreed with

I will now take the opportunity to recall the incidents and challenging situations that I faced over a long period of time and what eventually led to my resignation from the Labour Party.

The earliest incident following the demise of Councillor Wright and the need for a successor came (and bearing in mind I was the Depute Lord Provost for 2 years) when the three female Councillors in the Administration told me they had been approached by the Labour Party Secretary to put themselves up for nomination and stand against me in the forthcoming nominations to replace Councillor Wright. I was unhappy and very angry of course with this unexpected turn of events, but my faith in human nature was restored when my colleagues said they had turned the invite down saying I was the natural successor. I will always be grateful to them of course but I did hear the story that this request to "demote" me came from the highest level, a person who seemingly was of the opinion that if the SNP removed a women, the Party would replace her with another one.

My late wife Bette and I were like any other couple who had regular friends, and these friends would you believe became a contentious issue for my so called colleagues who objected quite openly that part of that group of six, two were Councillor Bruce Mackie and his wife Roberta who as everyone involved in politics will know are Conservatives. That became an issue as far as some of my Labour colleagues were concerned and comments like why do you fraternise with them they are Tories which made me very angry indeed and I have to confess that my replies were maybe confrontational and along the line that maybe I enjoyed their company more than theirs. Bruce has sadly passed away but Roberta and her family are still good friends and always will be.

Let me also enlighten you as to their attitude regarding Dundee High School.

I pride myself on the fact that I rarely if ever turned down an invitation as Lord Provost regardless of who or where it may have come from, I say rarely because I refused to share a top table with George Galloway once and there may be others which I am sure some readers may remind me.

Dundee High School was not one of these and when the invitation came through the letter box I was very pleased to accept. I might have to plead guilty to not sharing things, and I did not seek permission from the Party to visit the likes of Dundee High School whose Institutions might disturb the political dogma that engulfed the Labour Party on countless occasions, so I carried out my visit to Dundee High School and I was of course duly asked by senior Councillors as to why I accepted the invitation as it was a private School. I reminded them of course that Dundee children went to that School and I also reminded them that on the evening I was installed as Lord Provost I was quoted in the press as stating I WILL represent everyone in the City and this I did throughout my tenure of office without fear of any repercussions

I feel it necessary and amusing to tell you about the attitude and feelings of my visit to the High School that day and if the gentleman I have in mind is still around and reads this book I would be delighted to hear from him. At the conclusion of the Pupils Event we retired for tea or coffee and whilst standing with the Council Officer enjoying my tea and biscuit this elderly gentleman approached me with some emotion and said "Mr Letford I am so pleased to meet you and more pleased that you took the trouble to visit us here this morning, I thought I would never ever see a Lord Provost visit our School and you have made me a very happy man"

I said mischievously "I wonder why we have not visited before now" and his curt response "you will know better than me" said it all

If the attempts to remove me from the scene when I was Depute was an embarrassment then that embarrassment continued following what I believe was a Labour Party Executive Meeting in the Twinning Room. The Twinning Room or Lord Provost Reception Room is the responsibility of the Lord Provost as is the Civic Floor and for that reason I was surprised to enter the room to find the Leader of the Administration and the Director of Support Services carrying out an Inventory of the contents of the Twinning Room. I had not been given the details or the courtesy of their visit so I asked them what they were doing. The Leader told me they were taking notes of all "the rubbish" in the room, for example the Lord Provost Robes, a signed photograph of Tony Hancock the comedian and other choice pieces on their clipboard. I told them to leave the Twinning Room and informed the Chief Executive who must have spoken to them because they never came back, the fact that I was so embarrassed and ready to leave that day maybe had something to do with them not coming back as one less Councillor would have been bad news for the Leader. The Lord Provost Robes was an old story as the Labour Group had told me on more than one occasion I could not wear them at any forthcoming Event saying they had been banned and it was in the Council Minutes. The Lochee Legend Councillor Chic Farquhar told them otherwise and that the Robes had never been banned, there was no Council Minutes to that effect, and it was the Baillie's Robes that had appeared in the minutes and he was right of course, so I wore them then and after that as well. I should not have had to explain to them about the Tony Hancock Photograph to them, and didn't, if they had took the trouble attended some of the Civic functions in the City Chambers they would have been more aware of what was happening in their own City. I will however take the opportunity now to explain to you the reader of the very important circumstances that surrounded Tony Hancock's photograph.

I had on many occasions recognised the Blood Donors Association and their volunteers with a Civic Reception because of their exceptional lifesaving efforts but more importantly on that evening we celebrated the involvement of Dundee Royal Infirmary and their pioneering of blood transfusion and the interim involved all these years ago, and now 90 years of age was in the City Chambers that evening. Tony Hancock was of course the first person to give blood both here and in Aberdeen, hence the connection and history of why it sat with pride in the Twinning Room.

The intrigue and backstabbing was never far away within the Labour Party more so at election time and there was a disgraceful situation whereby pamphlets, unsigned of course were dropped from a white Triumph car in the Lochee area, the West End and the Hilltown decrying myself, Chris Hind, Jill Shimi and Fraser McPherson. I instigated a Police enquiry who investigated the issue and came up with so many cars that fitted the bill that it was impossible to trace. Had my sons mate had been quicker off the mark chasing him, after getting a leaflet through his door and got the registration we would have got the culprit for sure. That is not the interesting part of the story however because a very senior and well known person in the city, came to my office and told me, that when he was in the City Square he heard a sitting Councillor of the Labour Group boasting on how he had sorted out all the people who had been the subject of the nasty material being thrown from the car. The revelation came as no surprise to some of us in the Lochee Ward and no surprise he was stupid/ silly enough to seemingly implicate himself in this manner

I asked the gentleman who came to see me if he would be prepared to repeat the remarks he heard to the Chair of the Labour Party and he agreed. I followed this up by reporting this conversation to the Chair of the local Party and the Leader of the Administration, telling them this person was prepared to testify as to what the Councillor had said, but both the Chair and the Leader did not want to take action immediately because of the frailty of the Administration numbers, but would remove him at the next nominee meeting for the following election of the City Council. This did not happen of course and the Councillor in question is still a sitting Councillor which is another example of not supporting colleagues who had served the Party with distinction.

These events were the forerunner to the most challenging circumstances imaginable not only for myself but for my family and my dear late wife Bette.

On looking back to the events of that particular day that led to my resignation I made the mistake of asking the Chief Executive and the Director of Legal Services to come to my office so I could lodge a complaint against Councillor Keenan when I should have put my complaint in writing.

I say this because both the Chief Executive and the Director of Legal Services refused to confirm to the Press I had made a complaint based on the premise, as the Chief Executive said, that any conversation between him and a Councillor is confidential, and that was not helpful as far as I was concerned. Councillor Keenan denied that he had asked me to give the Depute the last 2 years of my tenure of office and he also denied that he had offered to get me an OBE if I agreed to his suggestion, however in the Dundee Courier of Friday 27th March he did concede that he suggested that "Mr Borthwick might look after someone who had given long service to the Council"

If that is not an admission of guilt then I don't know what is.

I was devastated that he thought so little of me or worse that he would "horse trade " in favour of Mr Borthwick and I asked him to leave my office as the conversation was ended. I suppose that was the straw that broke the camel's back and bearing in mind the previous intimidation and attempts to remove me I resigned and became an Independent Councillor answerable to no one other than the Citizens of Dundee.

I have to tell you that, that was one of the most challenging decisions I have ever had to make in my whole life and I did not do it lightly. I cannot remember when I joined the Labour Party but it was certainly many, many years before I became a Councillor and I mention that fact because some people join the Labour Party to make them eligible for selection as a local Government Councillor or indeed an MP whilst I and others who were Party activists for years would have certainly joined because of our activities in the Trade Union Movement.

I was a Youth Leader and an activist anyway in Charleston for years so it made sense to join the local Party Committee and I eventually became the Chairperson of the Branch in Charleston,

Gourdie and Menziehill. I have to say however the main reason I became involved in the Branch was through my Mentor and good friend Alec Craigie, Mr Charleston himself, a former Citizen of the Year and the one person throughout his life who did more for the area of Charleston and Lochee than all the other Councillors and Politicians put together, including myself, and now is the time to introduce the man himself.

Alec Craigie

Alec was of course a very special human being and was without doubt one of my closest friends not only in politics but as a Grandfather who's grandchildren played for Dundee Celtic Boys Club which I was a co-founder along with another close friend the late Dave Maillie.

My Mentor and good friend, Alex Craigie. Citizen of the Year with Bette and myself at the Chambers.

Alec was of course an intelligent, articulate, and well-read individual but he had a wicked sense of humour which gave me endless joy and fond memories of our time together.

Election campaigns for example were hard work and he and I put in many hours to ensure that the late Frankie Boag and the late Tom Mitchell, a former Lord Provost, were returned in the Charleston area and when it became my turn to be elected Alec was with me every step of the way, and many steps ahead of me if the truth be told, but that hard work was overshadowed by some hilarious moments which I will never forget.

We were "doing the rounds" in Brownhill Street in Charleston, me driving and Alec on the loud hailer with the well-rehearsed "vote Letford, vote labour" when we decided to put the hailer off and visit the nearby ice cream van of Frankie, who has by the way been delivering ice cream to the kids of Charleston, including my own, 50 years ago and at the time of putting pen to paper, is still going strong. If you are reading this Frankie, many thanks for being part of our lives.

Getting back to Alec, who had approached Frankie's van to be met with a torrent of abuse from a crowd of adult yobs, who thought they would have some fun at Alec's expense. Unfortunately for them, Alec's son Kevin came out of his tenement to hear Alec say "they're giving me a hard time Kevin". Now Alec's sons are lovely people but Kevin had a more fearsome reputation than Clint Eastwood's Dirty Harry and when the yobs saw who it was, they tried to scatter to the four winds running in all kinds of directions as their Nemesis came amongst them. There is always one who is not quick enough, so a right hook propelled him over a garden fence with Alec duly offering Kevin his "thanks son" and returning to the car and making short work of our ice cream cones.

The culmination of our campaigning was always the voting at the polling station, usually Charleston Primary and St Clements Primary school gates and Alec and I would either go to one or the other or we would share the same school handing out leaflets. On this particular rainy evening I returned to the Charleston Primary gates following a tea break and was concerned to see a police van at the gates and no sign of Alec. He was of course inside the van getting a dressing down from the police for poking an SNP activist in the chest with his umbrella. After the "bobbies" left telling him that he was a silly old fool, Alec said to me " don't worry John, there was no way they were going to arrest a one eyed pensioner" and as usual he was right and we lived to fight another day.

Alec's passion, enthusiasm, and determination was apparent one evening at one of my two Friday constituents surgeries at the Community Centre in Dryburgh, when on finishing at Charleston I headed for Dryburgh to join Alec who was "holding the fort" until I arrived. I got out of the car and could clearly see Alec and three young adults who were standing nearby, but because he was blind in one eye and had difficulty seeing me he shouted "is that you John" and when I confirmed it was me, he proceeded to chase the three yobs who had been tormenting him, down Dryburgh Street, flailing at them with his nearly full shopping bag. You have to imagine that scene if you can, which was like something out of Laurel and Hardy film, and once again Alec had made my day.

Alec as I said was my mentor and a political activist long before me and his advice was crucial as I started to get a political foothold in the Lochee area Charleston where I lived and although I eventually "rose through the ranks" to become a senior Councillor my first venture was a bit of a disaster because I did not take Alec's advice.

There was an impending nomination meeting in the Labour Party office to decide the candidate for the seat in the Menziehill area and I wanted to throw my hat in to the ring as they say but Alec said it was a bit too early in my career and he felt that the other Party member, a nice young man called Laurie O'Donnell was an ideal candidate and in any case had the backing of the Party. I insisted and wanted to test the waters and Alec reluctantly said he would support me and of course he was the only one of a dozen Party members who did. I learned a few lessons that bruising evening, firstly there is no substitute for experience, listen to people like Alec, learn, and prepare for the way ahead.

I remember Laurie well, he was a great Councillor, articulate, educated, and spoke his mind similar to Joe Morrow and Robin Presswood, all three ahead of their time and in opinion too radical and forward thinking for a Labour Party that was frozen in time with political dogma even now as it was then. I think it was in 1993 at a Labour Party Annual General Meeting that Laurie put forward the quite radical view that there was nothing wrong with an independent Scotland in tandem with a full autonomous Scottish Labour Party free from the shackles of Westminster and the National Party. I think he has been proven right and I share the view that Labour is unelectable in Scotland until they severe the ties with down south. I hope my memory serves me well Laurie, if not please forgive me and accept my apology!

In returning to Alec and myself and on a personal note, putting the politics aside, we shared a personal loss when we lost our dear wives, and in Alec's case we spent many of an evening together in Alec's house, talking about his loss, his grief and the years he spent with Ellen. Alec expressed a certain guilt, as we all do, that his voluntary work in the community and indeed throughout the City had taken him out of the house far too often, and he felt that he should have spent more time in the house they shared. I told him he need not have worried on that score because Ellen understood his passion for helping others and indeed supported him in everything he did and was very proud of him and what he did for the City which earned him a much deserved Citizen of the Year.

One of his sons said to me after I had resigned from the Labour Party that his Dad would have "turned in his grave" when I left, but I disagree. Alec was a passionate member of the Labour Party but he could always see others points of view and had absolutely no political enemies. I would like to think that although he would have been disappointed it would have made no difference to our friendship.

We will never know of course that if Alec were still alive would I have left? And the same thought goes through my mind at times, would I have left if Kate McLean or Jill Shimi had been Leaders of the Administration at the time. I was treated with the utmost respect when both of these very competent Leaders were at the helm so the answer to that one is probably no.

The Labour Party, both locally and nationally, is without doubt a different organisation now, that the one I joined all these years ago, and not for the better, it has in many ways lost its sense of direction and its social responsibility towards the ordinary people in our society and it seems to me that its heart and soul has been abdicated in favour of the Scottish National Party and I am sure this has been reflected in the massive turn of fortunes for the SNP locally and nationally and the subsequent massive drop in Labour Party membership in recent years.

My disillusionment and fractured relationship with my ex colleagues on the Labour Group was not an isolated incident as I have pointed out, but a series of events which started with my nomination and election as Lord Provost and continued throughout my tenure of office, and the distasteful suggestion that I should vacate my Office and seek an OBE was a step too far.

Those then were the reasons that made it impossible for me to work with people where mutual respect did not exist and if I am going to be consistent and perfectly candid, if people are seeking my demise, I am not going to roll over or turn the other cheek, I am going to survive and continue to serve the Citizens of Dundee in a manner they deserve. I think I did that.

Institutions - I

UNIVERSITY OF DUNDEE

In describing my experiences as Lord Provost it would be appropriate to recall my relationships with the Institutions that were responsible for all the good things and achievements of this beautiful City, not only at the present time, but in all the preceding years that enhanced the rich history of Dundee.

The tradition of the Lord Provost becoming a member of the Court of the University of Dundee is one I embraced with great enthusiasm particularly as I had been "spreading the gospel" about our Universities being a major force and without doubt one of the architects in transforming our City in recent years. I was extremely qualified in my opinion to put forward this point of view considering my past working history in the engineering and building industry within the City and I witnessed the demise of the Jute Trade, the Shipyard and other than the NCR and Michelin the manufacturing industries which fell by the wayside over the years but Dundonians being what they are, got up, dusted themselves down, and with the imagination and vision of the University of Dundee through their now world renowned scientists, Research, Life Sciences, investment and teaching Dundee became a potent force throughout the world. In all of these thing it is always about people, particularly young people and it gave me infinite joy to be present when the young people of both Universities and Dundee College graduated and the truth of the matter is I never missed one graduation in my 11 years as Lord Provost and my friends in the Graduation arena tell me that on a clapometer scale it makes me a candidate for the Guinness Book of Records.

With regard to the University Of Dundee Court and my input into their proceedings I have to say I enjoyed the experience on the occasions I was able to attend but attending was important and valuable for the City Council in knowing what their aspirations were and how we could assist where ever possible. I have to be honest and say that the duration of the meetings was somewhat long and not being an academic some of the contributions was heavy going like the day I had a difference of opinion with a lady during a discussion about the V&A. I apologise for not knowing or remembering who she was, but she asked the Chairperson quite indignantly what financial risks the University was incurring with their association with the V&A Project. I was incensed with her attitude because for a long time "everyone and their dog" including the University were claiming the plaudits for taking the Project forward, conveniently forgetting the man whose vision it was and I speak of the Director of the City Development, Mike Galloway. I informed the lady in question that the University was incurring no cost so far, costs would be incurred by the Dundee tax payers, and I was fed up with everyone else claiming credit for what was without doubt a magnificent opportunity for the City, and I am quite sure I saw Brian Cox giving me the thumbs up from across the table.

I had a wonderful working relationship with the University and worked with the Director of International Relations Joan Kingannon on many successful projects, but sometimes, things go wrong and on this occasion which I will describe the Director of International Relations got it very, very wrong.

A request came in from the University of Dundee through the Director of International Relations, Joan Kingannon for a Civic Reception in honour of a gentleman calling himself Prince Michael of Albany and Joan described him as the only living descendant of Bonnie Prince Charlie and therefore an heir to the British Throne. It was with some reluctance that I agreed to the request but because of our great working relationship with the University I granted the request and also agreed to go to his presentation event and question and answer arrangement at the University prior to him coming to the Chambers. His speech at the University did not please me at all and he continually referred to our Royal Family as Germans and how Scotland wanted to be free. He must have said this about a dozen times and I was first in line at "question time" to tell him he was talking nonsense and Scotland had always been free. I think he knew that I was a reluctant host at the Civic Reception and he got his own back by presenting me with a signed book about his history, his claim to the British Throne, and he wrote beneath his name "The truth will out" I consigned his book and his inscription to the bin on his departure and I have to tell you that I got it right and Joan Kilgannon got it horribly wrong as he was exposed as a fraud by the Brussels Authorities who had a copy of his birth certificate, stating he was born on the 21st April 1958 Michael Lafosse, his father being a shopkeeper, and his Mother being an employee. I have to tell you that the Principal Sir Allan Langlands was not impressed with the so called Duke of Albany and he told me in the Bonar Hall that the allegations about him were beginning to "filter through" and he had caught sight of the fraudulent letter that was to be undoing of Michael Lafosse and I got the feeling he was none too pleased with Joan Kingannon either. The last I heard of him was in 2006 when he lost his British Citizenship and was deported, did a runner and Interpol were chasing him across Europe. I am told now however that he has resurfaced and wrote another book The Hidden history of the Islamic Origins of Freemasonry. I don't know where Joan is now but that was not one of her better days.

My relationship with the University of Dundee was a very special one and I shared many happy occasions with Sir Allan Langlands, Professor Pete Downs and their staff at Graduations, Lectures, Receptions, and their sporting events at Riverside and at the Hawkhill Complex. I remember their Winston Churchill recognition being something special, particularly as the Council "bottled it" in not doing it themselves, in any event I was honoured to be there and pay our respects. The University of Dundee of course had great courage and did not shy away from contentious issues and Winston Churchill was only one of many. In my admiration for the University of Dundee and its Principals I worked with Sir Allan Langlands and his wife Elizabeth, and Pete downs and his wife also Elizabeth who were extraordinary and wonderful people, it was at the University in the Bonar Hall that I had the most unpleasant experience during my whole term of office!

I spent some time in a former Principal's office, not the two friends I have mentioned, prior to going to Dinner and there were three Professors and their wives along with the Principal and his wife in attendance with myself and the Lady Provost. The wives of the Professors were obviously in awe of the Principals wife and "butter would not have melted in their mouth" as the saying goes so the conversation was muted (football was not mentioned) we proceeded to the Bonar Hall where my personal "nightmare on elm street" was about to begin. I pride myself on being able to hold a conversation with anyone, but sadly I was teamed up with the Principal's wife for an half hour, I kid you not, and she proceeded to enlighten me about her academic life, her family's academic life, and of course her husband's academic life, until I was brain dead and honestly not remembering if I said a single word, she sat opposite Bette throughout dinner and did not speak to her once. She left before the end thanks be to God, the Professors wives relaxed and started to crack jokes would you believe and I breathed a sigh of relief.

The worst night of my tenure of office, without a shadow of a doubt, and unfortunately one I cannot forget.

If that episode was a disaster, and one of my worst memories, then the University gave me the opportunity to meet one of the most wonderful human beings, in my opinion, on the face of the earth.

That was of course Gary Player who was honoured by the University whilst I was Lord Provost and I had the great pleasure and indeed honour to meet the man and not the golfer! Mr Player spoke of his love for young people and his efforts on their behalf, his humble upbringing and his struggles to succeed. His early days in golf like the Carnoustie Open when he had no money, food, his trousers tied up with his tie would you believe and being befriended by a married couple from Carnoustie asking where he was staying. Finding he had nowhere, and taking him to their home and starting a life time friendship. His fitness, his clarity of mind and his determination is legendary as is his sense of humour. I was standing beside him when he put one of DC Thomson's photographers in his place when asked to do a photo shoot. When asked to "follow through" his swing after striking the ball the photographer threw a golf ball on to the grass lawn for the picture "What are you doing" said Gary "you realise I have just hit that ball on to the fairway" A sheepish snapper picked up the ball and beat a hasty retreat. That was a really good day for me.

The icing on the cake for me on a personal basis was of course being honoured by the University with an honorary Doctor of Laws in 2006 and that will be a prized possession for me in my life experiences.

Institutions - 2

ABERTAY UNIVERSITY

My first recollection of Abertay University was as the Project Manager of Community Industry, an Organisation that gave work experience to Adults and young people in both engineering and building construction. On the building side we cast concrete steps for house related projects and part of my duty was to ascertain whether the concrete mix we were using met the stress related requirements and to find this out I had to have them tested under high pressure conditions and that was where Abertay in Bell Street came into the picture. This was in the 80's of course and with limited visits which was to change when I became Lord Provost and attended not only the Graduations but the University itself where I met that human dynamo Professor Bernard King and shared many exciting projects not only in Abertay but in the City Chambers and on trips abroad. In my account of the Twinning Cities I did mention that Bernard accompanied me to Dubai where I witnessed at first hand his dynamic personality. He invited me to the University one evening to show me his pride and joy, the games industry and the amazing young people who put Dundee and the University on the world map in computer technology and after telling me the visit would only take half an hour I left some three hours later! Bernard was still there when I left of course and his staff told me on leaving that he would be there long after I had gone. I admired Bernard for his philosophy and his determination to support the less well-off students and make sure they got the same opportunities to learn and meet their aspirations. I was also recognised by the University for my contribution to Abertay and the City by being made a Fellow and I am honoured to still attend their present day Graduations on a regular basis.

Our relationship with the Universities known as Town & Gown is a historical one and although we value each other and recognise the importance of working together that relationship with Abertay was tested would you believe on a planning issue.

I was out of town on business unfortunately when the planning issue became quite serious regarding the Student Accommodation building at the bottom of Lochee Road which was considered by some Councillors, particularly the local Counsellor for that area, to be unacceptable and was turned down. Abertay were extremely upset about this and there was talk of them moving to Fife where they thought they would receive better treatment. We managed to avert this after some dialogue and a change of plan to the building height but the seriousness of the situation cleared the mind as they say and without breaching the planning code of conduct some forward thinking had to be considered.

The Chief Executive of the day, if my memory serves me well had already been thinking that Councillors had to be more pro-active in their determination to take the City forward and instigated a "meeting of minds" on a strategy of taking the City forward in a responsible manner. It was not only planning of course that should be on the agenda but a host of radical measures that would take us forward. In my opinion this was long overdue and it probably was a forerunner to the Changing for the Future which again in my opinion has been a great success and another indication of the expertise of former Chief Executive Mr Alex Stephen.

The legality and integrity of planning cannot be compromised of course but dialogue and consideration can be met prior to a submission I am sure and I hope that is what takes place.

ROYAL FAMILY

In addition to being Lord Provost I was of course the Lord Lieutenant representing Her Majesty the Queen here in the City of Dundee and because of that it gave me the opportunity to meet and welcome most, if not all of the members of the royal family which being a declared Royalist since my early youth gave me infinite pleasure and an insight in to what they were really like.

I first met Her Majesty the Queen in May 2002 here in Dundee as part of her Golden Jubilee Celebrations and found her to be the most beautiful person I always thought her to be, very

Her Majesty the Queen's visit to Dundee College and The Space Building - 2002

knowledgeable and a great sense of humour unlike the Duke of Edinburgh who on the first occasion I met him was very rude indeed. The protocol for the Lord Lieutenant on every Royal visit is to welcome them to the City, accompany them to their Event and move on ahead of them to the next appointment. I did this in May 2002 on the Queens Golden Jubilee visit to Dundee and her visit to Dundee College Space building and left early so I could meet her again at the top of Crichton Street before going in to the City Chambers for tea and cakes with our senior citizens. The Duke of Edinburgh was at the Welcome Trust with the Deputy Lord Provost Chic Farquhar and arrived at the top of Crichton Street before her Majesty and I welcomed him and remarked that he was early, he retorted "not me she's late" and proceeded to poke his umbrella into the metal gratings at the bottom of the tree at the top of Crichton saying quite disdainfully "you don't have very clean streets here do you" so right away he was removed from the xmas card list. The Queen duly arrived and we proceeded into the Chambers where she stopped at the bottom of the stairs to give me an account of the Burma

Star Plaque. I told her "you are very knowledgeable Ma'am" in my best creeping voice and she half turned looking in the direction of the Duke and said "that's him, he has me brainwashed" upstairs for tea and cakes and the Depute who was looking after the Duke's table said he was at it again when he was very rude to a Veteran when he discovered the origin of his medals were related to the Territorial Army. Following that meeting in the City Chambers I had the great pleasure to accompany her Majesty's to the Shore when she attended for lunch with the young people prior to her visit to open the newly refurbished Baxter Park Pavilion, a wonderful day indeed.

I met the Prince of Wales on three occasions, firstly to celebrate the historical Gardyne building restoration in the centre of the City, in the Great Hall in Stirling Castle, and in Grey Lodge Settlement at the Mary Lily Walker celebrations and on every occasion I found him to be charming, humourus and a great love for McGonagall. When I was introduced to him in the Great Hall of Stirling Castle as the Lord Provost of Dundee he could not stop laughing and said " Dundee, ah McGonagall what a man" I am sure he must have known McGonagall was born in Edinburgh but I was not going to tell him otherwise, so I just basked in the glory of getting the credit for the incredible bard who spent time in our City.

Having a laugh with 'Bonnie Prince Charlie' near Glamis Castle - 2008

Prince Andrew had none of the fine qualities of his brother and sister when I met him when he alighted from his helicopter at Dundee Airport en route to the Sea Cadets Base at TS Duncan in the Docks area. It was decided that I should travel in his car, driven by his equerry which was bad news for me as I had to listen to his tirade against a poor man who had no recourse to respond. It did not end there unfortunately and following his arrival at TS Duncan where he was inspecting the Cadets and witnessing their, in my opinion, very entertaining display I was of the opinion he wanted to be somewhere else. I may have misread his body language of course but I don't think so which is a great pity because it is the only occasion that I have been disappointed in the company of a member of the Royal Family.

I met Prince Edward on only one occasion whilst welcoming him at the University of Dundee Bonar Hall where he attended a musical evening performed by our young musicians and I could see he was pleased and comfortable to be in the company of young people, and he was himself a very presentable young man.

Princess Anne - You're my Favourite!

I have left my favourite member of the Royal Family to the last and for anyone who thinks I was disappointed that my MBE was conferred on me by the Princess Royal and not Her Majesty, not so.

In my eleven years as Lord Provost I must have had the great pleasure of meeting, and working with Princess Anne on at least eight occasions and the reason for that was her continuous visits and love for Scotland and the Tayside Region in particular. I came to know the Princess Royal quite well and found her to be a very determined Lady, intelligent, well read, and had always done her homework on the area and the people she met and did not suffer fools gladly. If you tried to be anyone other than yourself and had not your own homework she would suss you out quick as a flash. I witnessed the demolition of a Dundee Councillor at the Mills Observatory one day when he had not done his homework, did not know who he was introducing to her, proceeded to dig a hole for himself and could not stop digging, she gave him an uncomfortable afternoon in her company I can tell you.

I only saw the Princess bested in an argument once when an Irish lady, in my opinion got the better of a discussion about the culling of Badgers. This happened on the RS Discovery at a dinner in her honour one evening when the Princess Royal explained the damage that Badgers caused and why they should be "controlled" but this Lady from across the water had a Farm in Ireland and was in the habit of feeding strays including Badgers of course and it was a right ding dong I can assure you, amazing heady stuff it was. I did say she had a sense of humour but on one occasion it deserted her when she visited Dundee High School. I mentioned earlier the protocol of meeting and greeting before the event and when the Princess arrived that particular day it was raining of monsoon proportions and her official car went beyond the youngest line of pupils who were like "drookit rats" when she started to walk down the lines of pupils with myself trotting behind very dutifully, she overlooked the young kids. I proceeded to have a rush of blood to the head and committed Kami Kazi, and shouted, yes shouted, "Ma'am you've missed out the little ones their soaked to the skin" she turned round with an icy stare and said "Lord Provost we are all soaked to the skin"

On another occasion we met at the Unicorn, to which she was a regular visitor, and waiting for her to appear, I stood beside the President of the Combined Services Victor Herd, who let me see a wonderful little stamp book with a photograph inside of seven year old Princess Anne in a frilly dress. I asked Victor to give me the book and I said I would show it to her on her arrival which I duly did and it is one of my favourite photographs within this book. I got the feeling she was not "over the moon" with the photo and said something like "don't remind me Lord Provost of all those years ago!"

On the last but one occasion we met she said to me when I welcomed her to the City "not retired yet I see Lord Provost" and on the last occasion we met, I said to her "I've finally retired now Ma'am" as she presented me with my MBE and we had a wee laugh together, I will miss her.

NEW INITIATIVES

Any incoming Lord Provost, would I am sure, want to take the opportunity to instigate new initiatives, either on behalf of the City or on behalf of Individuals and I was no different, and each and every one I created, gave me great pleasure and an intense feeling of satisfaction.

I held the opinion many years before coming in to Office that Dundee was no less a major City than any of the others in Scotland and its Citizens in fact were the best and deserved to be recognised as such.

Christmas Lunches

I started first by introducing the Senior Citizens Christmas Lunches which was something very close to my heart because it gave the City the opportunity to give something back to our senior citizens, recognising all their efforts on behalf of the City over the years.

The Lady Provost and all her "happy helpers" Linda, Sheila, Rose, Carol, Ella and Edith supported me all my years in office and we all shared in having a great time with our Senior Citizens.

The entertainment for the Lunches was quite superb led by the Maestro himself, Ronnie Coburn of Breath of Scotland fame, an international star worldwide and a thoroughly nice man, who none the less did not suffer fools gladly and woe betide anyone who did not do the business. Ronnie was supported by Margaret Mather who organised all the entertainment with the young and the old over the years, and it was a great privilege to share my life with all of them.

Citizen of the Year 2006 and good friend Ronnie Coburn of "Breath of Scotland" fame.

I am absolutely certain that if Ronnie had not passed away I would still be with the Whitehall Theatre and with Ronnie by my side we would have taken the Theatre to new heights. The greatest tribute I have ever had in my life was to hear him call me his Pal, and if the great man said that to you then you really were his friend. I will never forget him and his friendship and what he did for his adopted City of Dundee.

Citizen of the Year Board

When I came in to Office my name was added to the Lord Provost Board in the City Chambers corridor and although it is an honour and a great privilege to hold this historical office there are other Dundonians who are more worthy to be honoured than ourselves.

It was for that reason that I introduced the Citizen of the Year Roll of Honour Board which recognises the many years of voluntary commitment to the City of Dundee and its Citizens. In addition to that it was disrespectful that not only was there not a Roll of Honour Board but there was no lasting memory of the great honour that they had received. I therefore instigated a Medallion that could be worn once their term of office was over.

The selection of the Citizen of the Year following nominations is carried out by many prominent people in our City from the Churches, the Universities, and the legal profession, two or three politicians and chaired by the Lord Provost. It is in my opinion the most democratic process I have ever been involved in and thankfully the politicians are in a large minority.

The Citizen of the Year Board personifies all that is good about the ordinary Citizens of Dundee and we should all be very proud of those who have been recognised.

Dundee Youth Council

I have since my early days as a Youth Leader and my youth training years with Community Industry Rathbone, a youth training organisation, been committed to the development of young people and recognised their aspirations to play a part in society, so following the success of a Youth Conference Day during the week of our Twinning Cities visit to Dundee and at the Shore Building I asked the Leisure and Culture Department and the participants from Youth Voice to visit the City Chambers to explore the opportunities for creating a Youth Council that would have an important and official part in the development of our City, and have official recognition from Dundee City Council.

I chaired the early meetings until the young people themselves were in a position to create their Organisation and elect a Chairperson. The young people have worked hard and produced many interesting and major Reports and Surveys reporting on the needs of young people within the City and putting forward their own views on how the City should be taken forward. I have to say that other than the Alexandria Twinning Committee, the other Twinning Committees have not been enthusiastic and this is disappointing as the young people want to be involved. I have often said that some adults do not listen to our young people and it will be an opportunity missed if Twinning does not encourage our young people to join them. Although it was not a new initiative I worked very closely with all the youth organisations in the City as their President, namely the Boys Brigade, The Girls Brigade, The Girls Guides, The Scouts, The Brownies and the Anchor Boys, all wonderful organisations and very important to the City of Dundee.

City in Bloom

On my travels across Scotland, and in particular Perth, which was just "up the road" I was always impressed with the floral display on view that seemed to light up their City Centres and the approaches to their City and I mentioned to the then Chief Executive that I thought we as a City were the only one with a Direct Labour Department and should be leading the way in floral beauty.

We had the usual banter about costs but as usual he "came up with the goods" and a three year financial plan was devised by himself and his Officers and not only was the City Centre in full bloom but the beauty throughout the City was a joy to behold. It is little wonder that we are now considered quite rightly as a beautiful place to be but the appropriate and only City with a Flower and Food Festival.

Open Doors Day in the City Chambers

Once a year there is an Open Doors Day throughput the City where businesses, Churches, Public Buildings and various Organisations and Institutions take the opportunity to open their doors to the public whereby they can gain entry free of charge. It is extremely popular with the people of Dundee and of course Dundee City Council themselves in a Civic sense opened their doors and in all cases I think the exercise is very well attended. I took the opportunity to attend the Chambers on these days to meet and greet the people of Dundee over a cup of tea and biscuits in the Twinning Room and on occasions I would attend in the Chambers and do the "five bob tour" myself. I found this very rewarding, so much so that I suggested to the Staff that we should do this on the last Saturday morning of every month. The Staff were agreeable and I was most grateful because that day may have been the only day they had off that week, it turned out to be a huge success and amazingly it was often the first time that some people had ever been in the City Chambers, this was a great shame because factually the Chambers was theirs. We did this for some considerable time and it then tapered off, maybe because we had other commitments but at the time of my retirement we were no longer carrying out this very important service

Lord Provost Youth Parade

It is not difficult to recognise my feelings for the young people of the City in my book and I hope that certain events in my tenure of Office demonstrates this also, no more so when I introduced the Lord Provost's Youth Parade to coincide with the visits of young people from Orlean France, Alexandria Virginia, Wurzburg Germany, and Nablus Palestine.

Lord Provost Youth Parade

There are many Parades that have taken place in this City over the years but to me there was no comparison that matched 700/800 of our own youngsters representing Clubs, Community Organisations and voluntary groups from across the entire City marching through our street to the City Square culminating in displays of dancing, singing and all the activities that our kids are involved in every day of their lives.

A wonderful day to cherish all their lives but sadly another experience no longer with us because we as a City have retreated. "possibly in the face of austerity and the cuts that are all too prevelent in these troubled and financial times."

I had, in my opinion, a nice wee phrase for my staff, forgotten now in the mists of time I suppose, "Don't tell me why I can't do it - tell me how I can do it"

SNP

My earliest recollection of the Scottish National Party by way of identifying with them was prior to the 1990's when I visited Dundee City Chambers with Councillor Chic Farquhar who was a Dundee District Councillor and my Boss at Dundee Community Industry, an Organisation that gave work experience to young people and adults. I had met MP Gordon Wilson at my place of work in Community Industry when he came to visit our youngsters and I was extremely impressed with his commitment to young people and to the City Of Dundee in general and over the years as the SNP Leader and to the present day his honesty, integrity and care for Scotland has never wavered. He is of course a Rotary colleague and keeps me focused on the rights and wrongs of politics.

I came to love the very historical and magical atmosphere that exists in the City Chambers and even then I thought that this was the place to be. Those were the days of the huge Labour majority that had existed for decades in Dundee Corporation and Dundee District and at that time I started to visit on a Monday evening for their Council Meetings when out of 32 elected members my memory tells me there were only 3 SNP Councillors (maybe 4) namely John Corrigan, Jim Smith and David Coutts. They gave a good account of themselves but the Labour Group Convenors were very rude to them, cut short their allotted time to speak and yet would let their own colleagues speak forever.

The storm clouds were gathering however and all this was about to change

In the early 1990's I was elected on to The Tayside Region Council only to be in the Opposition when the SNP were successful and Frances Duncan became Convener. The 2 things that stood out in my memory of their first day in power was the half black and half yellow dress that Frances wore and the removal of the Union Flag from the Tayside House Building. That was one of the many mistakes that Administration made, because we had it back within hours.

I have to say that as an Opposition we did quite well and bizarrely I think we enjoyed the experience of being in opposition of harassing them at every turn and we had many successes notably rubbishing their "light bulb" fiasco which was declared illegal I think, their sacking of all the cleaners which we reminded them of continually and many more. We also knew that many of them had commitments in the evening so we prolonged Meetings and it's amazing how we got our own way in the end because they all wanted to go home! I don't want to be too unkind to them but they were, fortunately for us, not as competent as the present Administration of Dundee City Council but, never the less, very nice people.

The storm clouds I mentioned had arrived in the City politically with a vengeance and the steady rise and election successes of the SNP was dramatic and it made no sense, and demonstrated how much out of step they were in Scotland that the Labour Party nationally were feeding us with junk mail, warning us of the danger of the Conservatives with little or no mention of the real danger on our doorstep, the Scottish National Party. The junk mail of course along with the pictures of Tony Blair, if we are all going to be honest, ended up in the bin or were stored in our garages, and Joanne Lamont got it spot on when she said Scotland was only a branch office

The resignation of Councillor Joe Morrow and the subsequent by-election in the Maryfield Ward was said to have signalled the end of the Labour led Administration when the SNP won the seat but in my opinion the writing was on the wall much earlier. I was given the credit, or the blame, of their demise after the Dundee City Council Meeting of 30th March 2009 but it depended which side of the fence you were standing on, or indeed depended on the way Members voted that evening, let me explain.

Following the Maryfield by-election which gave the SNP 14 seats, One short of an overall majority, I was approached by a representative of the SNP to advise me that they were going to call for a special meeting of the Council to replace the present Administration with themselves because 3 Members of the coalition were going to abstain and they were going to propose that they intended to leave the Lord Provost and the Depute Lord Provost in place. I advised the representative that I would have to advise the Labour Group of our discussion which duly took place.

The Labour Group rejected this of course indicating that the Labour Group would select their own Lord Provost and not the SNP and that concluded the discussion and was I thought, the end of the matter.

I have already described my reasons for resigning, but not for voting for the SNP on the 30th March and I will do so now. The local Press in some small detail reported on my discussions with my family on this matter, but not in great depth, so I will take that opportunity now.

I had taken every opportunity to inform my immediate family of what I intended to do on that evening which was to abstain from voting and I will never forget the discussion I had with second Son Graham over a cup of tea in Morrisons. It was going smoothly for a while as it had done with the rest of my family, and like the others I had his total support, until I mentioned abstaining.

I was shocked at his anger when he said "why are you abstaining?" and when I told him there were others who would do the same he said, "Dad I don't care about the others, you brought us up to say what we think and do what we thought was right, regardless of the consequences,

I don't care who you vote for but I will be disappointed in you if you abstain" and as a parting shot he said "have you ever abstained" and the answer was of course, no. It was a rude awakening I have to tell you to be reminded of my own principles, and I told him that I could not vote for the Labour Group and it would be the SNP and he said "I don't care as long as you vote"

I did vote and never regretted it, so thanks Graham and the Dundee City Council Meeting of the 30th of March did in fact have 4 abstentions One more than the SNP Representatives had predicted so they did have that information and in fact did not need my vote on the evening in question.

In the interests of being honest and consistent, which I have endeavoured to do throughout this book I will not insult your intelligence and say I did not have a discussion with the Leader of the SNP Administration following the evening of the 30th March, which I did, and that frank discussion resulted in myself reserving the right not to support them on a matter of conscience or any Independence issue brought up in the Chamber. I was never asked, but they knew, I would not put their Administration in jeopardy, and they, for their part, allowed me to carry out my Civic duties without interference.

On a personal note I think they have done an excellent job in looking after the wellbeing of the City and I am not ashamed or embarrassed to admit I am pleased they were given the opportunity to "see what they were made of" and I also think they will be around for a long time.

I did attend one of their group meetings but felt extremely uncomfortable and did not repeat that again throughout my term of office.

WHITEHALL THEATRE

My first introduction to the Whitehall Theatre was in the early 1980's as an employee of a Company called Community Industry when we refurbished and redesigned the Caledonian Church to become an extension of the Theatre as it is today. The driving force and the man behind the Project was the late Mr Bill Crowe, a gentleman if ever there was and one who was to become a very good friend. It was Bill who asked me one day if I would like a couple of tickets for a show and being a "boatyaird man" and a film buff I originally declined on the basis that I thought the Theatre was for "toffs" . I am pleased to say he persuaded me to attend and that was the start of a life time love of the Theatre. In the early 1990's in addition to being the Personnel Convenor of Dundee City Council I became quite naturally the Liaison Person between the Council and the Theatre and a Member of the Whitehall Theatre Trust.

I remember only too well the visit to the Chambers by the then Chair of the Whitehall Theatre Trust Norman Robertson seeking help because of a very large financial deficit in the Theatre's budget and although we could not clear their deficit, we paid for the new seating in the Theatre out of the Common Good Fund. I did however suggest involving the Theatre with our Education Department which would ensure some stability for the Theatre. Many people within the Education Department have claimed credit for the new found relationship with the Council, the Theatre, and in particular the Dundee Schools Music Theatre at that time but I can assure you that the Chair Mr Norman Robertson, myself and others had the major role in all of it. In fact if the truth be told about the origin of schools theatre the Evening Telegraph of 29th of May 2000 tells us that Margaret Mather of Dundee Junior Showtime was the creator of Primary and Secondary Schools performing in the Whitehall Theatre and that it would be the forerunner of the future, how right they were.

As I said there were others who played a major role in all of that, no more so than David Strachan who was recruited by Norman Robertson to be the Administrator of the Youth Theatre also known as the Whitehall Youth Theatre Guild. The years between 1996 and 1998 was to see shows and rehearsals, all at the Whitehall Theatre during school holidays with the first one under the direction of Lesley and Terry Whale the husband and wife team from the Perth Theatre with the Musical Director the legendary John Scrimger. There was lots happening under the leadership of David Strachan and in 1997 the Whitehall Youth Theatre became a satellite group of the National Youth Music Theatre of London which had the support of Andrew Lloyd Webber, all heady stuff would you not agree. The 1997 years show I believe was "Tongue Cut Sparrow" a Japanese fable with the production team all from London with David's son Ian doing the musical rehearsals. It is interesting to remember that all the props for the show were made by the stage director and a group of Dundee kids. 1998 was to see the demise of the Youth Theatre but not before the production of Calamity Jane directed by Tony Ellis and once again musical director John Scrimger both from Perth Theatre.

David Strachan's legacy and his administration expertise was paramount in all that was created in those early days and following his prudent financial expertise the partnership between Dundee City Council was helped on its way when in 2002 the Council allocated funds matched by the Whitehall Theatre Trust

It is well documented that the Theatre fell on hard times which culminated in the demise of the Whitehall Theatre Limited which did not manage the Theatre to a level that would ensure its success and because the Whitehall Theatre Trust eventually, after continuous bail outs, ended loans that were never repaid, it was obvious that the Trust would get criticism for the Limited Company's shortcomings. The then Chair Derek Shaw handled this criticism well and with the full support of the Trust, of which I was a member, protected the Theatre's future and called a halt to the handouts which were putting the Theatre in jeopardy.

The survival of the Theatre was imperative and Derek Shaw worked endlessly to make this happen, and Derek and I met with Dundee City Council to negotiate a support package that would ensure the Theatre's survival and we were successful in taking this forward. I disagreed unfortunately with Derek on how the communications of the Trust should be taken forward and after he left, on a sound financial footing I have to say, and I took over as Chairman, I was to find out that he had got it right and I had got it wrong. To explain that, I had always thought that the procedure of taking decisions should be done through regular Trust meetings and not by emails, but that can only be successful if all Trust members are making a contribution, and so I found myself, like Derek Shaw being the only one, other than the Treasurer Alex Scott, spending all my time in the Theatre on a daily and weekly basis, and when I asked for help from the Trust members to share this daily basis arrangement none was forthcoming and it was little wonder that I doubted the value of the Trust members contribution.

The outstanding problems required to save the Theatre was the extensive refurbishment and Health and Safety issues that needed attending to, and I can assure you this was a major undertaking involving thousands of pounds, and the Council's part in all of this was to support us in providing a Venue Coordinator who was in fact my Council Officer Davy Barr whilst I was Lord Provost. If anyone can be credited with getting the Whitehall Theatre back on its feet, it was without a shadow of a doubt through the efforts of Davy whose working hours in the Theatre went way beyond the call of duty. At the time of reading this Davy will be back on duty in the Council Chambers and the Whitehall's undoubted loss will be the Council's gain.

The time I spent in the Theatre was very rewarding but long and arduous and my family were for ever giving me "stick" reminding me that I was now retired and should be enjoying life, the truth of the matter was I was enjoying myself as long as "idle hands" left me to get on with it. My time as Lord Provost was of course beneficial for the Whitehall and my many good friends within the Council, and the many Institutions and Organisations particularly the Charity Trusts throughout the City responded to my call for help to the tune of many many thousands of pounds.

In order to get the support of the Council and their Venue Coordinator however, there had to be a commitment from the Amateur Groups in the City to use the Theatre, the Volunteers to give their support, which was never in doubt as they are the life blood of the Theatre and its existence, and last but most important the Education Department who promised to use the Theatre. There was agreement from all concerned but after the Service Level Agreement was signed the Education Department reneged on their commitment and made it very difficult for us to proceed.

The unusual situation of having two members of the Education Department on the Trust was not helpful as they obviously had a conflict of interest and indeed were not working in the best interests of the Theatre, and if the truth be told the Council at one point said to me that they had a conflict of interests, but failed in my opinion to address the situation and the conflict continued with the only physical help coming to myself from Alex Scott and Judith McMurray the Chair of the Whitehall Theatre Cub.

The refurbishment however was taken forward successfully, to the satisfaction of the Fire and Rescue, the Police, the Council and other Regularity Bodies, the expertise of Susan Gillan of the Caird Hall delivered an abundance of Entertainers and Shows and the future of the Theatre looked good.

I felt because of this progress being made it was the appropriate time to recruit new members for the Trust that had business acumen, financial expertise and a knowledge of the Theatre that would take the Whitehall Theatre forward in to the future. I included my position of Chair in this reconstruction but the other Trust members excluding Alex Scott did not support this point of view and wanted to return to the system that had put the Theatre in jeopardy.

In conjunction with these proposals was my suggestion to donate £1000 to the Scout movement and the Gang Show who were struggling at that time to put on their show but the Education member on the Committee objected to my style of Chairmanship regarding this, the Trust members agreed with him, and because of these two circumstances I took that to mean that the Trust had no longer confidence in my leadership. So I immediately resigned.

With regard to the Scouts Gang Show and the donation I had proposed with the full backing of the Treasurer Alex Scott, who pointed out to me that our constitution had a requirement and a budget to cover my proposal, I have as the previous Chairman, in fact seen the Trust's financial figures that indicates that a previous Trust and some of the present Trust members had previously donated thousands of pounds, as I have described, to the Youth Musical Project here in the City, and yet objected to supporting the Scouts Gang Show, quite cynical don't you think?

In looking back over some 30 years involved in the Whitehall Theatre, I have many fond memories and although I feel let down by people I thought were my friends, the politician in me understands how people can change when their perceived status is threatened. I left the Theatre in a better condition in which I found it and Derek Shaw, Davy Barr, Alex Scott and I can have no regrets regarding the efforts we put in to keep this iconic Theatre alive and I can look back with great pleasure working with some of the people I have mentioned. I wonder if the present Trust is at peace with themselves as we are?

LORD PROVOST JOHN ROSS LETFORD

On the 25th June 2001 I had the great honour to be installed as the 32nd Lord Provost of the City of Dundee and although the circumstances surrounding my appointment were not as I would have wished, the opportunity to restore some dignity to the role of First Citizen was a challenge I relished.

Although there have been 32 Lord Provosts since Alexander Mathewson in 1890 the history of Civic Heads of the City goes back to 1286 with Radulfo as Magistrate, and thereafter Baillie's and Provosts 275 in total over a period of 728 years.

Twinning (Orlean)

My Senior Council Officer Gordon Williamson once suggested to me that if I had a legacy to leave as Lord Provost it could well be that of fostering and improving our relations with our Sister City Twinning arrangements worldwide, ensuring that young people become the focus and important part of Delegations visiting Sister Cities worldwide and ensuring that visiting Delegations to our City include young people and I hope I have achieved that aspiration.

Our first and oldest Twinning City of course is Orlean France which was formed in 1946 and is indeed the longest Twinning partnership in all of Europe. The protocol and first point of contact in all of our Twinning arrangements is always the Municipality and the Mayor. The invitation process for Orlean is always for the Joan of Arc Festival which prior to my retiral, no invitation from Orlean had been received for at least four years, which is quite disappointing but I have to say that as a City we continue to invite them annually as we have done since I took Office. The Joan of Arc Festival is a wonderful spectacle, participated in by many thousands of residents and of course visitors who simulate Joan's successful siege of the City with a four hour walk around the City with a stop at the bridge across the river Loire to lay wreaths in memory of the three hundred Scottish archers who died protecting Joan of Arc against the English, and on one of these many walks I did I was accompanied by French President Chirac, who only lasted one street by the way and was off in his helicopter. The other unforgettable experiences were of course the simulated siege of the Orlean Cathedral which was spectacular to say the least, and the wonderful singing choirs in the Cathedral, a building which has been made famous with the saying and advice of "remember to take your coat because it's freezing in there" and the historical beggars outside all with their designer clothing and fancy trainers! There were negatives to our visits to Orlean as well of course mainly because I have always maintained that Orleans attitude to twinning was not shared or was as enthusiastic as ours. The Mayor for example would meet us on arrival at the City Hall and meet us as we said goodbye with no contact in between. There was no twinning committee as such in Orlean and visitors to Dundee were usually Councillors who in the main stayed together except for one visit and that was a great pity because of Orlean and Dundee being the oldest and longest Sister City

Twinning Partnership arrangement in Europe. We did have the Auld Alliance Organisation in Orlean who worked tirelessly to highlight everything that was Scottish of course and they were extraordinary people who loved Scotland and paid many visits to Dundee themselves. On one visit myself and our delegation were invited by The Auld Alliance Organisation to witness the unveiling of a Street Plaque commemorating all those Scots who died in the war against the English, and when invited to speak I found myself going into a tirade against the English, which came as a bit of a shock to the Dundee Delegation, Conservative Councillor Rod Wallace, myself included of course because I am known to be a strong supporter for maintaining the Union and the United Kingdom. The makeup of our visiting Delegation was always the Lord Provost, Lady Provost, Senior Council Officer, and a Senior City Councillor and in most occasions four Students who could, or were, learning to speak French. There were of course other exchange visits out with the Lord Provost's Office which included the Rotary, Schools, Coral Singers and good friend Anne Lore's Pipe Bands and although the official invitations had stopped these other activities continued over the years I was in Office.

Twinning (Wurzburg)

The Wurzburg twinning arrangement formed in 1962 was a different and a more productive partnership and although they like Orlean did not have a twinning committee they had an ex council employee called Karl Schmidt and his wife Erne who organised visitations to Dundee and looked after us when we visited Wurzburg., but again like all our Twinning communications the first point of contact is always the Municipality and the Mayor's Office. In my particular case in 2001 it was Pia Beckman who was of course a female and in the early years again like the French was not ever enthusiastic about twinning and would greet us on our first day and then sees us off at our departure and on one occasion provided a Deputy. I took this to heart, and considering the welcome and friendship offered to them when they came to Dundee I sent her a letter suggesting she required training in the art of Civic Protocol, and that did the trick, a confidant in her office emailed me to say the " Ubberburgermeister" had said to him "It appears I need training in the art of Twinning according to the Provost" and sure enough the relationship was transformed, Pia brought her guitar with her on visits, sang in both German and English and was great fun and even mastered " twa pehs eh bridie an an ingin ina" we were all so happy we named a street called Wurzburg Drive in the west end of the City but believe it or not it caused a political storm when the location was destined for the Stobswell area, so much so that we changed the system of street name selection which I think has went by the wayside at the present time.

The then Mayor of Wurzburg Georg Rosenthal and his lovely Wife Hannah, who I worked with for some time is without doubt the most enthusiastic and committed politician that I have met from Wurzburg with regards to twinning and his respect for Dundee and its citizens is amazing which is evident in his visits to our City and the amount of time he and Hannah spend with us when we visit. The invitation from Wurzburg on a yearly basis is to attend the highly prestigious

Mozart Festival in the magnificent Bishops Residence which was almost totally destroyed in the Second World War but also totally restored by local tradesman and it is regarded as the most iconic building in Europe. In speaking about the bombing I cannot help but remember the most amazing, and forgive me for saying, amusing conversation myself and the Senior Council Officer, Gordon Williamson, during dinner in one of our visits to the largest wine Cellar in Wurzburg, The Burgerspeital, when a stranger at our table who had too much wine, and with his head in his hands said to Gordon "why, oh why did you bomb us", and a slightly agitated Council Officer who served in the Royal Air Force said "because you bloody well bombed us first" you could not make that up could you!

I had the great pleasure to be invited by Mayor Rosenthal to Wurzburg after my retiral, to celebrate their 40th Anniversary Celebrations little knowing what was in store for me! At the celebration event in their City Chambers (Rathous) there was a great musical presentation by Wurzburg Musicians and Dundee Musicians billed as "The Bridge" and to my surprise and great delight I was welcomed officially and described as "The Bridge" for the Twinning between Dundee and Wurzburg and for my contribution over the many years I was in Office and if that wasn't enough I was gobsmacked to be presented with their yearly Peace and Friendship European Award "The Dancing Shepherd". I hope to return to Wurzburg sometime in the future so I will have to brush up on my German which I used in the 70's and the 80's when visiting Cologne to participate in Youth Football. The Senior Council Officer Gordon Williamson always reminded me that we both attended University to brush up on our French and German and he finished the whole course and I didn't, I'm sure he had more time than me!

Twinning (Alexandria)

In recalling my tenure of Office as Lord Provost and Twinning, Alexandria Virginia has been very special for many reasons but one in particular has been the inescapable fact that of all our Twinning Cities Alexandria is the only one with an active Twinning Committee made up of ordinary citizens whose sole purpose is to support the City of Alexandria in the ethos of Twinning, peace, friendship and the understanding of each other's culture. The official invitation from the Mayor's Office and the Campagna Centre was to attend the Scottish Christmas Walk held in the streets of Alexandria on the first Saturday of December each year led by the Saint Andrews Society followed immediately after by the Dundee Delegation who has pride of place not only because of the Twinning but because Alexandria is a City with a Scottish heritage which is very evident by the display of tartan which is not matched anywhere else in the world. It really is a magnificent experience and following a more than three hour walk around the "blocks" Dundee has pride of place once again by being on the large stage for the March Past of every Group and Organisation taking part and Dundee's Lord Provost always gets the opportunity to address the very large gathering. The other honour that came our way one year was for our very own Army Cadet Jennifer Mainds the Lord Lieutenant's Cadet for 2008/9 to play solo on her pipes at the finale and indeed we had four Dundee pupils with us that year and a later year nine members of the famous Dundee Schools Musical Theatre who performed not only in Alexandria but in Washington DC, a great honour for the kids and a great honour for the City of Dundee. In all of the wonderful places of interest I have had the good fortune to see the Abraham Lincoln memorial is probably my favourite not only for who he was, but what he stood for, his memorable speeches and his leadership in the American Civil War. I am a bit

Dundee Alexandria Twinning visit to Washington for Annual Scottish Christmas Walk in Alexandria.

of a Civil War buff and courtesy of the St Andrews Society I got the opportunity to visit some of the battlefields, including Georgetown, Fredericktown, and most importantly Gettysburg. It took exactly five hours to travel round the Gettysburg battlefield with our very knowledgeable guide, and I stood on the very spot where Abraham Lincoln gave the Gettysburg Address, and my host, Douglas Brooks President of the St Andrews Society Washington, knowing that my grandson John James collected stones (at that time) gave me a piece of rock from the "Little Round Top" where the decisive part of battle was won. I have to add that with regard to my hero Abraham Lincoln I had the sadder occasion of being in the Ford Theatre where he was shot and I was in the house he was taken to and I stood at the very bed in which he died. It was not to be the only places of interest that Douglas would take me, and knowing me to be a sheet metal worker to trade he organised a trip to the Sheet metal Workers Union establishment in Maryland, which was to make me famous or infamous in the Maryland, Alexandria, and Washington areas. On the previous evening at an intended visit to the White House some of our youngsters failed to bring identification with them and were refused entry and although I had my visa with me I would not go in without them and missed out, but wait, the best, or worst, has still to come. The following day I was in Maryland on my way to the Sheet metalworker's Union building when Douglas received a call and said "it's for you from the White House" well! It was a lady from the White House right enough saying "we are sorry you missed the White House visit last evening but if you would like to come today President Bush will be in the Oval Room and you can meet him" I thanked her for the invitation but explained I was committed to the arrangement with the sheet metal workers and could not let them down, five minutes later the same lady phoned Douglas again asking to speak to me, "Did you not understand my message? I said the President would meet you in the Oval Office" I told her I did understand her message but I was otherwise engaged and she put the phone down! Absolutely true I assure you and I was subsequently accused of snubbing President Bush, now would I do that.

The exchanges between Sister Cities Twinning as far as Alexandria is concerned has been extremely successful with young people from Schools in each City travelling back and forth annually with Projects of an academic nature, music, culture and through all that activity friendships have been forged that have stood the test of time. I was successful in having the support of the University of Dundee who sent scientific researchers on cancer to the Maryland American Institute Of Health and the surrounding States including Alexandria Virginia in 2009 to take part in a major Health Conference. It did not end there however and we have adult rugby teams competing against each other for the Mayor of Alexandria Cup on a regular basis. There is of course an historical link with Alexandria, the United States and Dundee long before the Twinning came on the scene, and that is of course the Jute Trade. The covered wagons that were all too common on our TV screens, the ones the Indians kept burning down (I've always said they were Dundonians in disguise looking for new orders) were made here in Dundee's jute mills and provided important trade to our City as did the sails of the John Paul Jones ships in America which were also made here in Bonnie Dundee.

I am pleased to say that Alexandria and Dundee have another exciting partnership arrangement between Dundee & Angus College and Nova College and that arrangement has been expanded to include the Dundee Alexandria Twinning Committee of which I am the Secretary.

In the first chapter of my book I said I would be honest and forthright and I am not going to dodge the issue by hiding the fact that Alexandria, their Twinning Committee, and the people of that City have by far. given me the most wonderful experiences of any Sister City over the years. When I started out in my tenure of office I had only a short period of time working with Mayor Kerry Donald as Bill Euille was about to replace him as Mayor and Bill and I started our Terms of Office about the same time. This was to be good for me as I was not an ardent admirer of Mayor Donald and Mayor Euille was to become one of my best friends and I had the great pleasure of working with Bill and Rose Boyd throughout my time as Lord Provost. Our first point of contact as a Sister City is always the Civic Head or City Hall but the inescapable fact is that in any Sister City it is with the ordinary people, the Twinning volunteers, that lasting friendships are made. I did not have the pleasure of working with Linda Whitton as Chair of the Alexandria Twinning but I did work with Sue Brooks, Mary Jo Johnson and the present Chair Maureen Duggan which has been a very rewarding experience, and although I retired in 2012 I have taken the opportunity to visit on more than one occasion and I will continue to do so as often as I possibly can.

Twinning (Nablus)

Of all our Sister City Twinning arrangements, Nablus, formed in 1980 was I suppose the most controversial, and presented the Dundee Nablus Twinning Committee with the most difficult challenges far beyond anything experienced by Orlean,Wurzburg and Alexandria and it is a great credit to the Nablus Committee that they have retained their commitment and passion for over 30 years. I am sure few would argue with the view that the Twinning arrangement with Nablus was of a political nature and it had a difficult birth with the Palestinian Flag being burned in the City Chambers and the City being divided in its creation. There is of course a myth that there is no Palestinian Flag in the City Chambers, untrue, a Flag has been there on the Chambers stairs as far back as I can remember and in addition to this I ensured that there is a similar Flag on the rooftop of the Caird Hall. We have of course survived these bad experiences and although exchanges are almost impossible DNTA members over the years have managed to overcome the difficulties put in their way by not only the Israeli authorities but the Jordan authorities as well.

I would be less than honest if I were to say the Nablus Twinning arrangement did not present me with difficulties as Lord Provost, for example, I was never able to visit Nablus because on two occasions the Foreign Office advice was not to travel because of the escalating conflict, the Twinning Committee had no such reservations however and some members visited when it was possible for them to do so. The Chief Executive of the day and myself always thought I could travel before I retired but for various reasons I was not able to carry out that duty.

It was not always plain sailing between myself, the Director of Legal Services of the Council, and the DNTA and although it took a few years to resolve (thankfully we did) we did manage I think to impress on their Committee that I could not put forward a political view on the Israeli/ Palestinian conflict, regardless of their view that only the Israelis were committing atrocities. We were determined to hold the view that our Twinning Associations were created to promote peace and friendship, highlight each other's culture and remain non-political, and therefore our Twinning Committees had no remit to promote a political view, and I was obliged to inform the Foreign Office that the Dundee Nablus Twinning Committee did not represent the view of Dundee City Council

I always hoped that my attitude towards not "taking sides" as the Civic Head of the City did not mean that I was oblivious to their deep passion for the plight of the Palestinians, I did understand their passion and frustration and indeed on many occasions criticised the Israelis for "disproportional responses" and the UK Government and the United States for not trying harder to solve the Israeli/Palestinian Conflict and had they provided this commitment I was sure peace in the Middle East would have followed.

We have had on occasions, visitors from Nablus of young people, Musicians and of course the magnificent Fire Fighters of Nablus who I welcomed and entertained in the City Chambers with a Civic Reception and our own Fire and Rescue Service through Jim Malone and his colleagues have been superb in providing training and physical help with Fire Appliance equipment. All these events and efforts including the young people who have eventually made it over here to Dundee were supported by the Nablus Twinning Committee and the University of Nablus and to date the Dundee Nablus Twinning Committee continues to be as committed as they have ever been over these many years.

Dubai

Our Twinning arrangement with Dubai was somewhat different than our other Sister Cities and more of an economic venture and for that and other reasons which I will explain later and with the approval of the then, Chief Executive we transferred the partnership to the Economic & Development Department later to be renamed City Development. The invitation to seek a formal Twinning arrangement came from the Al Maktoum Institute for Islamic Studies and it's then Principal, Professor Al Awaisie who on behalf of HH Sheikh Hamdan Bin Rashid Al- Maktoum, Deputy Ruler of Dubai and the United Arab Emirates, Minister of Finance and Industry, and Patron of the Al-Maktoum College of Higher Education. Prior to the Official signing of the links with Dubai in 2004 I led a Delegation to Dubai with Professor Al-Awaisie, Director of Economic Development Doug Grimond, Professor Bernard King of University of Abertay, ex Lord Provost Merv Rolfe, (others) with the intention of exploring the possibility and the opportunity of a twinning arrangements between Dundee and Dubai.

I have to say that our intended visit met with some resistance and a Council Meeting had to be arranged to get approval for the visit and to discuss some of the reservations that some Members had. I did my homework of course and found that Dubai and the United Arab Emirates were considered to be the most moderate of all the Arab States and did indeed meet the most serious concerns that we had, that of recognising equal rights for woman, so in the end the Meeting approved the visit almost unanimously, and I say almost because the late Councillor Julie Sturrock wished her objection recorded. I used to describe Julie as the last true socialist because she would never, and I mean never, compromise her caring philosophy towards the ordinary people in our society and her reticence to vote for the Dubai visit was to justify her way of thinking later on in my tenure of office.

Councillor Julie Sturrock was not the only person to have serious concerns at the proposed Twinning with Dubai because Mike Arnott the leading light of the Dundee Trades Council had registered his concerns to me that Dubai did not allow Trade Unions and therefore they were opposed to the Twinning taking place. I could relate to his point of view because of my trade union background, but as Lord Provost I had to consider the anticipated financial benefits that I was being advised would come our way, and we will have to wait and see if Julie and Mike got it right and I got it wrong. In all of our visits to Dubai we were treated with great respect and being "treated like a Lord" comes to mind. The Staff at the Sheikh Al Maktoum's seven star hotel addressed me as Lord Letford for the duration of our visit and Professor Al Awaisie told me to accept it rather that confuse the hotel staff. I had the Royal Suite of course, three bedrooms, two Jacques's, a grand piano in the lounge, rose petals daily on the floor, in my slippers, on the bed and would you believe in both toilets, it's a hard life being Lord Provost I can tell you.

In the Sheikh's small Palace I looked out into the sand dunes one day and saw what I thought to be Jockeys, trainers on a string of horses and being a know all I said to the Sheikh, "Is that Frankie Datori and your horses Excellency" and with a little smile on the corner of his mouth he said "Lord Provost these horses are camels" well you can't win them all can you. We were on another day treated to a day and a night in a hotel in the desert, saw the sun go down at dinner and then total darkness, and I mean total darkness, up next morning for a camel ride in the desert (an absolute nightmare on the back of a camel I assure you) and half way round glasses of Champagne on a sand dune with waiters in tuxedos and ladies in evening dresses.

Next stop Abu Dhabi, a welcome from the Ruler in his Palace and off to a French Hotel for lunch (he drove himself in his jeep) where we nearly had a seven course meal, I say nearly because the Sheikh didn't finish any of the courses and when he decides to go, he goes, and everyone has to go with him and poor Ernie Ross MP who had ordered a special vegetarian lunch had to go just as it came to the table. It was the custom for us to have a Delegation Meeting at the close of day to discuss how the trip was going and prepare for the next day and the evening of the Abu Dhabi visit with Sheikh Khalifa bin Zayed Al Nahyan, something extraordinary happened between Professor Al Awaisie and Principal of Abertay Bernard King.

The Professor and Bernard King were not bonding well on the trip, the reason I will explain later, and they were discussing the Sheikh Al Nahyan when the Professor said the Sheikh was liable to take out his gun and shoot a person if the need arose, a statement that shocked the Delegation but more so Bernard King who went "hammer and tongs" with the Professor. I am sure he must have been winding us all up? I hope so!

There was one not so nice experience and it happened at the British Ambassador's Residence with the Ambassador asking a question about the camel races which were outlawed in Dubai because of the habit of tying young children to the camels, which the Ambassador said was still going on, and following the question the Arab Diplomats said the practice was unlawful and they walked out.

As far as the Twinning arrangement was concerned I made the decision to cease our twinning arrangements because I had asked Dubai through the Professor and his successor Prof. Mallory Nye for permission to start a Twinning Committee here in Dundee and they refused. There is a commercial arrangement with Dundee City Development but I do not know the status of that arrangement at this moment in time.

In looking back at the relationship we had with Dubai the one outstanding achievement we had as a City was my request to Sheikh Hamdan bin Rashid Al Maktoum to consider direct flights to Scotland via Glasgow and this was granted in 2008 when I had the great honour to be invited to Dubai and return in the very first flight to Glasgow and Scotland. We never really got the credit we were due for this major coup for tourism and Glasgow being Glasgow milked it for all it was worth, you can't win them all can you.

National Anthem

I have to confess I had a major disagreement with the Principal, Malory Nye of Al-Maktoum Institute for Islamic Studies regarding our National Anthem. My Council Officer had informed me that at the visit to the Marryat Hall of the Depute Ruler of the United Arab Emirates Shaikh Hamdan Bin Rashid Al-Maktoum, the National Anthem of both Dubai and Scotland would be played. "I smelled a rat" on this one and asked the Principal what tune they would play for Scotland and was duly informed that it would be Flower of Scotland. I told him of course that I would stand up for the Dubai Anthem but would remain seated for Flower of Scotland. I also informed him that as the Lord Lieutenant of Dundee and representing Her Majesty the Queen there is only one National Anthem for the United Kingdom and it is not Flower of Scotland.

I don't think he believed me but when I sat where I was, he was aghast as was the Depute Ruler of the UAE and all the SNP Councillors who were sitting in the front row.

DC THOMSON

I have long held the view that sayings like "there is no substitute for experience" or "don't judge a book by its cover" have been relevant in my own life experiences and in many of my own situations have been absolutely true, and I am thinking of DC Thomson in particular, as a glaring example of my way of thinking.

Coming from a background of the Unions, the Labour Party, Engineering, Shop Stewards, etc., there was a perception that DC Thomson were Tory, anti- Labour and that a "them and us" culture was the order of the day.

This was nonsense of course, but at that time it was convenient for us to blame "someone else" for the ills of the world and DC Thomson I think were at times in the firing line. I cannot claim to be the one to change an antiquated state of mind, and bring some sanity back in to our relationship with the local press, but there was change coming in the shape of people like Robin Presswood, Joe Morrow, and former Lord Provost Mervyn Rolfe, and when I became Lord Provost with a remit to highlight all that was good in our City I joined this august group of forward thinking intelligent people and my first incursion in to this new way of thinking, at the behest of Merve Rolfe, if my memory serves me well, was to give recognition in the Chambers to a retiring Editor of DC Thomson. (Hope I got that one right Merve)

That was only a beginning of course and myself and the Chief Executive met with the Thomson Family Board when the need arose to share dialogue on the challenges that we as a Council faced in our decision making process, and for their part, an understanding of their business strategy and at the same time accepting that they would print what they thought was in the public interest.

On a personal note, and respecting the confidentiality aspect of our relationship I can only say that their support for the Civic Head and the City itself was quite magnificent.

I was of course invited after my retiral to write my column which was a wonderful experience and although I was replaced by a "younger model" I was given the opportunity to "speak" to the City I love, and I will always be grateful to DC Thomson for that.

RETIREMENT

I use the term retirement very loosely because I am very pleased that I am fit and able (fingers crossed) to continue with many of the activities I have been involved with over the years, and I carry out Secretarial roles for the Dundee Alexandria Twinning Association, I hope to visit Alexandria in December and meet all the friends I met as Lord Provost, also Secretary of Lodge Forfar & Kincardine. As the Patron of SSAFA and the minute secretary I work with others to raise funds in order that soldiers, sailors, airmen and their families can get the benefit of our efforts, particularly through the annual SSAFA Concert in the Caird Hall.

Don't cry for me 'Argentina' : Davey, Gordon, Bill and Ashley.

I am appropriately, because of my age, an honorary member of the Pensioners Forum here in Dundee, a member of the advisory committee of the Order of St John, of which I am proud to be a Commander, and last but not least the Chairman of the Ways & Means Committee of the Rotary Club of Dundee.

I do of course still get invites to go to events from many of the Organisations I was part of when Lord Provost and I am pleased that this includes both Universities of Dundee and Abertay, not only for their most interesting and informative events but more pleasing attending their graduations.

If that is retirement then I am very happy to be retired.

On my last day in office as Lord Provost and preparing to leave after saying my goodbyes to staff, my Secretary Ashley said there was a problem with the lift that took me down to the underground garage and TS1, and I had to leave by the main entrance to take me to the top of Crichton Street where TS1 was waiting for me.

Last day at the Office. Farwell from 225 Medical - 2 May 2012

I have been on many occasions been able to work out or suspect when "surprises" lay in wait for me but on this particular occasion I did not have a clue. I was gobsmacked to find that I had a guard of honour from the entrance to the City Chambers to the top of Crichton Street by her Majesty's Armed Forces through which I was escorted to the civic car, a very emotional experience I can assure you.

I cannot finish an account of my life and time as Lord Provost of the City of Dundee without thanking the wonderful people on the civic floor for their commitment, support and indeed friendship that made my tenure of office an absolute joy. Ashley, Stuart Galloway and his staff, the Council Officers, and the ladies in the kitchen, all of them looked after Betty and myself and gave us the utmost respect, we were indeed a family and we loved sharing our lives with you all.

There was of course the dark days which were very challenging and I could not have got through them were it not for a young lady called Ashley, who not only steered me through my civic duties but held me together when I lost Betty. I will be forever in her debt and love her always.

It is amazing what you can manage in a lifetime, in a city that has given me a wonderful family and love and friendship beyond my wildest dreams.

THE END...